DESIGNING
TERRY PRATCHETT'S
DISCWORLD

'Typical artist,' said Granny.
'He just painted the showy stuff in the
front. Too proud to paint an honest
potato! [. . .] And what about these
cherubs? [. . .] I don't like to see little
babies flying through the air.'

'They turn up a lot in old paintings,' said
Nanny Ogg. 'They put them in to show
it's Art and not just naughty pictures of
ladies with not many clothes on.'

'Well, they're not fooling me,'
said Granny Weatherwax.

DESIGNING
TERRY PRATCHETT'S
DISCWORLD

PAUL KIDBY

HARPER

An Imprint of HarperCollinsPublishers

For Vanessa, with all my love and thanks for
working with me on this book.

With thanks also to Rob Wilkins, Alex Stott, Harry Hall, Suzy Smithson and Heather McDaid

CONTENTS

FOREWORD 6

MAKING IT UP AS I GO ALONG 9

CHAPTER ONE
JOURNEY INTO DISCWORLD 11

CHAPTER TWO
CRAFTING A UNIVERSE 25

CHAPTER THREE
THE WIZARDS 31

CHAPTER FOUR
THE WITCHES 67

CHAPTER FIVE
THE ANKH-MORPORK CITY WATCH 85

CHAPTER SIX
DEATH AND WHAT COMES NEXT 129

CHAPTER SEVEN
TIFFANY ACHING AND THE FEEGLES 161

CHAPTER EIGHT
GODS AND HEROES 177

CHAPTER NINE
MOIST VON LIPWIG AND ANKH-MORPORK 195

CHAPTER TEN
FAR-FLUNG LANDS (*forn parts*) 215

CHAPTER ELEVEN
OVER THE EDGE 225

CHAPTER TWELVE
THE STUDIO ENVIRONMENT 235

CHAPTER THIRTEEN
PERCHANCE TO DREAM ... 245

AFTERWORD 252

PICTURE CREDITS 254

FOREWORD

At the turn of the millennium in a small town in Northern Ireland, a boy stood in a bookshop with a £10 note in his hand and studied the rows of spines in front of him; he was about to do something he'd never done before in his life – he was about to buy his first book with his own hard-earned money. It wasn't his first time in that bookshop, he'd been visiting it for weeks, always drawn to the same shelf that was lined with a particular set of volumes that somehow called to him. He reached forward and slid out the book he had already decided to purchase. At the counter, he handed over his £10 note, pocketed the change, walked home, sat on his bed, opened the book and began to read.

The book was *The Colour of Magic* by Terry Pratchett.

The boy was me.

Fast-forward twenty years: far from that small Northern Irish town, there I was, sitting in an audio studio in central London, headphones on my head and a microphone before me. I took a breath and began:

'*The Colour of Magic*, by Terry Pratchett, read by Colin Morgan.'

In the twenty years between those two events, the boy had certainly become a man; but when I read those words in that audio studio in 2022 I was whisked back to 2001 and felt the same spark of excitement I felt as a teenager, a feeling of love, of coming home, of starting a whole new adventure.

Since opening that first book, I have devoured every single Discworld novel I could get my hands on and, being a purist, I read them chronologically by release date. Through my teenage years and into my twenties I collected the entire series and those original purchases still sit on my shelf to this day. They are treasured, adored, and always manage to stoke a pang of childlike joy in me at the prospect of starting one all over again. What was it about these books, this world, these people, this author, that struck a chord with me at such a young age? The escapism: from my world and onto the Discworld? Yes. Away from the inhabitants of Earth and into the company of those Discworld dwellers? Of course. Tickled by the wit of the author and comforted by his constant presence taking my hand and leading me on the journey? Definitely. It was all this and much more, perhaps something fans of anything find hard to pin down and make sense of. When I read those books I felt a connection and experienced a kind of awe: that a human being could put words on pages and weave such intricate tapestries in my head. When I discovered Terry Pratchett I found a fellow traveller into the realms of fantasy. Terry was the man with the key to every door and I walked through them all. He was like a master chef of the imagination and he served up course after course of pure . . . well . . . magic.

I've always had great admiration for those who have the ability to funnel the masterpieces in their heads onto paper; I stand in open-mouthed amazement at these blessed individuals. Terry is one such. Paul Kidby is another.

My mouth is rarely ever closed when I set eyes on his work. When I say 'master craftsman', or 'gifted beyond measure' – I don't feel like I've even begun to scratch the surface of suitable descriptors for Paul Kidby. There is, quite simply, no one like him. As a Discworld fan I feel so lucky and proud to have him as our city planner, our population manager, our forestry and wildlife ranger, our universal architect: in fact – I'm going to say it – a god.

Actually, on a very personal and special level, he is a kind of god to me – for he quite literally gave me life on the Discworld itself; he gave me a body, a place of my own to live for ever to walk amongst the characters I had imagined for so long. There was only one requirement from Paul to make this come true: my face. Let me explain . . .

It was during the recording of the audiobooks of the Wizard series for Penguin Audio that I was delivered the overwhelming news that Paul Kidby had based one of his creations on me! What?!

I couldn't believe what I was hearing! Me?! The boy who always wished he could be in that world had been inaugurated onto the Disc?! It was a 'pinch me' moment! Which, oh which fabled character did I have the truly incredible honour of being immortalized within? Tell me!

A Goblin.

Namely, Of The Twilight The Darkness.

Now, some may deflate slightly at that avatar selection; not I! Never has a man leapt so high with joy at seeing his own features on such a gnarly little creature. I delightedly contacted Paul and told him not only how bowled over and honoured I was to be Of The Twilight The Darkness, but also what immensely high esteem I held him in, what devotion and admiration I had for his craft. Even via email I could tell that Paul was a very modest man: he thanked me in that fashion and asked if I would mind being his muse for another character he was thinking of. Would I mind?! I told him I'd be doubly honoured all over again!

This time I would receive an upgrade. To a god, no less! Yes! Which god?

Bilious, the oh God of Hangovers (well, we can't all be Blind Io, can we?). (In fact, this choice of deity was probably more appropriate than Paul initially thought as I was born on 1 January, which could be described as the unofficial feast day of hangovers.)

As Paul began work on Bilious he sent me photos of the process in sketched pencil form and I could not believe this was happening to me. When I saw a photo of the finished, coloured painting I was actually speechless. I don't know how long it took me to try to compose an email to Paul expressing my delight – that the boy in the bookshop was now a god of the Discworld – the feeling is beyond compare.

Imagine then how it felt, on a lunch with Rob Wilkins to celebrate the completion of the Wizards audiobook series, when he handed me the framed original painting. I'm not going to try to describe the moment; by now you may have an inkling of just what that meant (and means) to me. Bilious hangs on my wall and every day when we lock eyes I'm suddenly fourteen again.

Paul Kidby has enriched us Discworld readers by visualizing the landscapes of our imagination, he has put before our eyes the world we love to visit and perhaps long to live in, he has brought further to life the characters we know and love, and he has paved roads that allow us to walk throughout Discworld. He continues to do this with a quiet modesty, a humble brilliance and a unique virtuosity. What is to come in these pages is a celebration of the ever-expanding body of work Paul has created. So be prepared from here on, for the awe you will experience will have the side effect of leaving you constantly open-mouthed; please dress accordingly.

Thank you, Paul: thank you for it all and thank you for what is to come.

Colin Morgan
London, May 2024

MAKING IT UP AS I GO ALONG . . .

It was a joy to work with Terry Pratchett. He was an encouraging and enthusiastic collaborator.* As a working illustrator, all I could afford to focus on was the job in hand, but looking back I'm aware of the trust Terry invested in a young artist, and the huge honour it was to be able to illustrate his creation.

The concept of this book has taken me a few years to become comfortable with. This is because I often cringe when I look back at my early Discworld drawings and I have had to be persuaded to dig them out of the vault and share them in the public eye. However, I can see a visual timeline runs like a red wire from the early work, through the decades, to my current renditions. Nobby and Cohen might look rudimentary in the early designs but the basic premise of their characterization and conceptual DNA can still be seen in my recent drawings of them. People sometimes ask me if I ever get bored drawing the same characters and I can honestly reply no, because every time I put pencil to paper, I am pushing myself to refine and improve what has gone before. Much as a professional musician constantly rehearses the same piece of music – the challenge is to constantly strive for better.

This book shows my visual design journey and how the characters have been developed over the years – from sketchy drawings on cheap paper by a hungry young artist to the more refined work that has taken me decades to develop. I hope seeing my process and my humble beginnings will help to inspire and encourage the next generation of illustrators.

Paul Kidby
The New Forest
May 2024

* . . . as long as I got things 'right'!

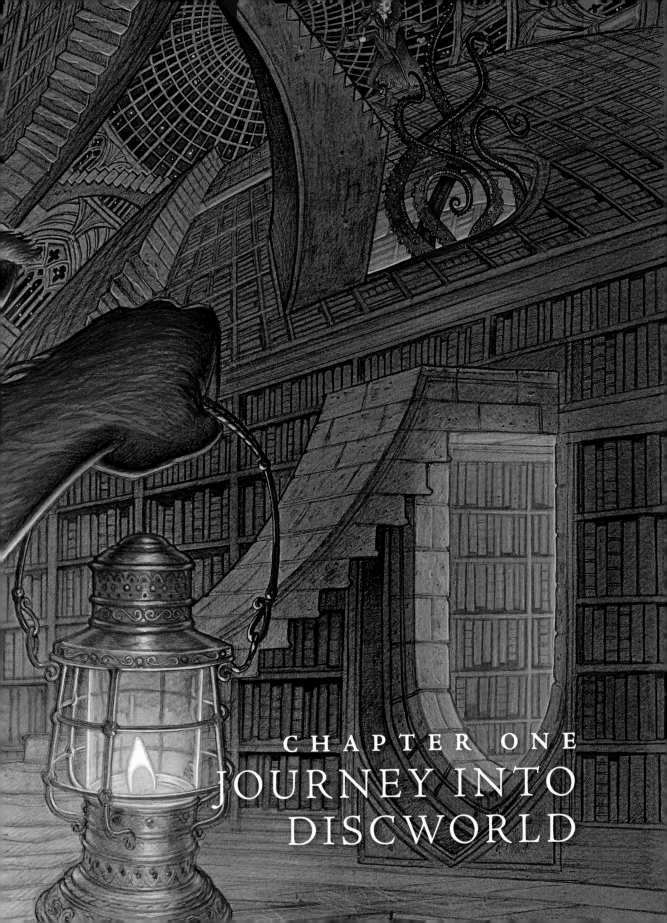

CHAPTER ONE
JOURNEY INTO DISCWORLD

Me aged 8

My dog, Pip, drawn from life when I was 12

A copy of a Neave Parker T-rex drawn when I was 10

DINOSAURS AND DOGS

I spent my childhood in the borough of Ealing, in West London. I was much the youngest of three creative children. Having a father who was a stationery salesman meant there was ample supply of paper and pencils and I always spent time at home drawing and modelling with plasticine.* My first forays into published art were for the Barantyne Primary School carol concert programme, followed by the termly school magazine, and the *Mirror* newspaper where I entered a drawing competition titled 'Outside my Bedroom Window'. I drew Islip Manor Road and then, for good measure, added dinosaurs. It won third prize. The accolade of being in a national newspaper was secondary; my main excitement was duly receiving the coveted prize of plastic toy dinosaurs.

*and trying not to annoy Mum by getting it stuck in the carpet!

An unusual angle of a brontosaurus by Neave Parker, c.1955

I was always blessed with an over-active imagination and it became vivid at night when I would lie in bed convinced dinosaurs were outside my bedroom door. I enthusiastically collected the prehistoric animal cards that came in Brooke Bond tea leaves: I loved the miniature illustrations that were gently scented with tea. Another passion were the art postcards of dinosaurs by naturalist illustrator Neave Parker.

For a while I thought I would be a palae-ontologist when I grew up. My interests soon expanded to include geology and – as with every other kid my age who watched the moon landing on TV – astronomy.

My sister introduced me to the Charles M. Schulz *Peanuts* comic strip. From then on, I loved Snoopy, and I also discovered the comical work of Norman Thelwell. Both artists were able to capture a character and make me laugh with a few strokes of the pen. So began a new enthusiastic phase for me, which turned out to be my lifelong passion – drawing.

Researching and taking inspiration from artists through time has been – and still is – an important part of my creative development. No idea comes from a cultural void; everything has a starting point and it is interesting to track artistic influences across the decades. For example, the early twentieth-century German artist Heinrich Kley influenced Walt Disney, and Georges Braque inspired Picasso. Nowadays I am equally flattered and amused to see my own work referenced by art students as part of the process of developing their own unique style.

My homage to Snoopy, one of many drawn at primary school

Film poster for 'Monty Python and the Holy Grail.'

DOING THE FOOTWORK

missing, but was a not-so-subtle indication that there was some commercial value in art.

At one point I successfully interviewed to become a postman, but pulled out at the last moment. Had I not done so the visual aspect of Discworld as we know it now might never have been realized by me.

Not being trained in art and art history, with life more focused on popular culture than on the Royal Academy, gave me a certain freedom of approach. I broke the rules because I was unaware of them. At one point in my teens I stopped painting altogether because handling paint had led to so many disasters; it was only when I invested in some decent watercolours rather than my set of basic poster paints that things began to go better for me. Also, looking back, MDF might not have been the best choice of surface for large paintings. Yet I was never put off for long by mishaps with materials or financial challenges and my overpowering ambition was always to earn a living through art regardless of the challenges it presented.

When I was thirteen, I bought a copy of the script of *Monty Python and the Holy Grail* which included line drawings by Terry Gilliam. They were amusing, intriguing and bizarre. Inspired, I bought myself a Rotring fine liner pen set and started to emulate his style.

The realization that drawing could be funny, weird and tell stories without words was a journey that I wholeheartedly embarked on and am still enjoying every bit as much today.

My early artistic career took an unorthodox path that did not follow a formal art-school training.

As an under-qualified seventeen-year-old school leaver I initially worked in a dental lab sculpting false teeth, on the Youth Opportunity Programme (a job I secured on the neatness of my handwriting). My professional path then led me to painting designs in a roller blind factory. During my tenure, the factory was broken into. The only things taken were abstract canvas paintings of lightning and geometric shapes that my co-workers and I had created for fun using the industrial-grade airbrushes available to us. This wouldn't be the last piece of my work to go

Coincidentally, I've drawn false teeth numerous times illustrating Discworld characters. You never know what will prove useful in the future . . .

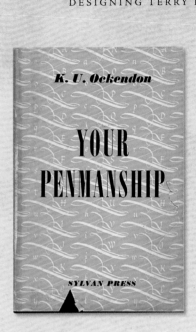

K. U. Ockendon

YOUR
PENMANSHIP

SYLVAN PRESS

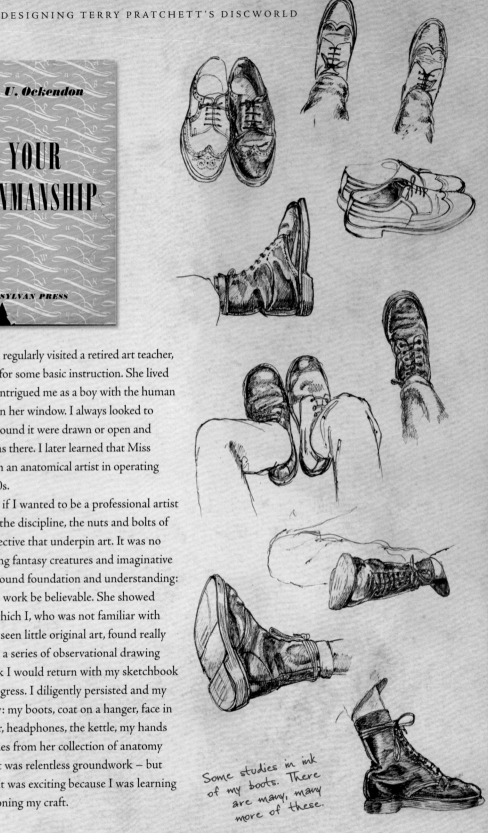

In the early 1980s I regularly visited a retired art teacher, Kathleen Ockendon, for some basic instruction. She lived on our road and had intrigued me as a boy with the human skeleton that stood in her window. I always looked to see if the curtains around it were drawn or open and wondered why it was there. I later learned that Miss Ockendon had been an anatomical artist in operating theatres in the 1950s.

She told me that if I wanted to be a professional artist then I had to learn the discipline, the nuts and bolts of anatomy and perspective that underpin art. It was no use, she said, drawing fantasy creatures and imaginative subjects without a sound foundation and understanding: only then would the work be believable. She showed me her own work, which I, who was not familiar with art galleries and had seen little original art, found really inspiring. She set me a series of observational drawing tasks and once a week I would return with my sketchbook and show her my progress. I diligently persisted and my pile of drawings grew: my boots, coat on a hanger, face in the mirror, headphones, the kettle, my hands and studies from her collection of anatomy books. It was relentless groundwork – but for me it was exciting because I was learning and honing my craft.

Some studies in ink of my boots. There are many, many more of these.

FROM JURASSIC PARK TO UM BONGO

By the late eighties I was working for a graphics studio in Thornton Heath creating packaging and greetings cards, including for some early video games such as *Sidewinder*, a sci-fi shooter game. Designing greetings cards required me to complete three paintings a week. I created renderings of sports cars, electric guitars and Walkmans, all at top speed – not to mention a foray into promotional packaging for Um Bongo. The relentless deadlines and short lead times further instilled a sense of discipline in me – there was no time to second-guess – I had to get things right the first time.

A move out of London to Somerset was the stimulus for the next phase in my creative career and in May 1991 I took my portfolio to show a panel of editors at Future Publishing at the invitation of Kevin Hibbert, art editor of *PC Format* (who I had initially met in Bath's legendary 451 Comics). They received

The artwork for 'Sidewinder', one of my very earliest video game paintings

my work positively and commissioned me straight away. By June I had created my first magazine cover, for *Commodore Format*, issue 9, titled 'Hack Attack'.

The next four years I worked exclusively for Future, creating a huge quantity of magazine covers. My paintings could be spotted in newsagents on *PC Gamer*, *Your Sinclair*, *Commodore Format*, *Amiga Power*, *Sega Power* and *Games Master*. Characters such as Catwoman, Sonic the Hedgehog, Earthworm Jim, the Terminator, along with Jurassic Park and an award-winning Batman cover all got my treatment. The Batman cover actually won the award for art director Wayne Allen, a plaudit I never begrudged him; like Terry he was the best sort of collaborator – generous in scope and not overly prescriptive, something I find always yields the best results.

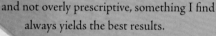

Um Bongo, Um Bongo, they drink it in the Congo . . . allegedly.

During these years I produced one magazine cover a week and used a variety of media and techniques including oil paint, acrylic and airbrushing to achieve the bright, vibrant designs necessary to meet the brief. In fact, I threw in every trick in the book to get the work done within the deadline. It was good if relentless training.

Illustrating famous characters felt like a step up from working on commercial packaging, where I'd served my time painting illustrations for light bulbs, rice pudding and sailing boats. However, what I really wanted was to design my own, original interpretations of characters.

Earthworm Jim

In what little spare time I had, I was working on designs for characters from J. R. R. Tolkien's *The Lord of the Rings*, with an ambition to ultimately create a hand-painted graphic novel adaptation. Then I saw Alan Lee's work. Somehow, he'd reached the ideal, perfectly realized version of Tolkien's world. It was a moment both devastating and truly inspiring. Everything felt perfect – the costumes, the environments, the armour – I didn't feel I could better it, but it showed the power of illustration to tell a story.

In a strange narrative echo, I illustrated a festive Grim Reaper the year before Terry wrote 'Hogfather'. This one is a little more sinister than his Discworld counterpart . . .

My airbrush was indispensable, but also frustrating, as it had a tendency to block and splatter on my artwork and I seemed to spend as much time cleaning it as I did using it.

An orc who, alas, never made it to Middle Earth

19

FLIGHTS OF FANTASY

I n 1993 my sister Linda posted me a copy of *The Colour of Magic* by Terry Pratchett for my twenty-ninth birthday. I read the story and then looked at the cover by Josh Kirby. It was a classic Kirby, riotous, colourful and detailed. Josh had had a long and impressive career illustrating movie posters and book covers since the 1950s and he had been creating the Discworld jackets for Terry since 1984. I, however, imagined Terry's characters differently. Josh's work for Discworld was both frenetic and stylized, a tone that perfectly captured the energy of the novels – but I felt left space for a more grounded interpretation.

Not long after, I got word that *PC Gamer* magazine was going to be running a piece on Terry Pratchett and the man himself was coming into the Future offices for an interview. I collected photographic samples of my work, showing character designs (of orcs, elves, skeletons and warriors), and put them in an envelope with a letter introducing myself. The editor agreed to pass it to Terry. The message came back that Terry had been complimentary, but nothing came of it. I realized that if I wanted to really pique Terry's interest, I had to

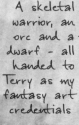

A skeletal warrior, an orc and a dwarf – all handed to Terry as my fantasy art credentials

In a distant and second-hand set of dimensions, in an astral plane that was never meant to fly, the curling star-mists waver and part . . .

THE COLOUR OF MAGIC

draw his own Discworld characters rather than the generic fantasy drawings I had submitted. I went to Hunting Raven bookshop in Frome and bought more Pratchett paperbacks and got reading . . .

I then began to design and draw the characters from Discworld; I created Rincewind, Cohen the Barbarian, Nijel the Destroyer, Granny Weatherwax, Nanny Ogg and Magrat. Once again, I wrote a letter to Terry and put copies of my pencil illustrations in an envelope. This time I posted it to Terry's publishers, Victor Gollancz. There was no reply.

Still undaunted (and bloody-minded), I bided my time. I kept creating magazine covers for Future, and further developed the Discworld designs. In due course I spotted a poster in the window of WHSmith in Bath advertising that Terry was coming to sign copies of *Men at Arms*. It was a grey day on 19 October 1993 when I launched my third attempt to gain the author's attention – this time I would place the artwork in his hand myself. On arriving I was surprised

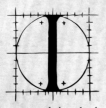

An early wizard design for 'Commodore Format' magazine in 1991

20

My first professional oil painting created for computer game packaging. In the absence of models, I resorted to the Littlewoods catalogue for Will Scarlet (with mullet) and Maid Marian (in her nightie). Robin Hood himself is me (with hair!).

by the size of the queue which weaved around the bookshelves; I had not quite grasped the popularity of Discworld! A couple of hours later my turn came, my book was signed, and I handed Terry another manilla envelope filled with copies of his Discworld character designs.

'This is for you,' I said.

'To keep?' asked Terry.

'Yes.'

And that was that, my moment with the author was over and for the next few weeks I resigned myself to it having been a hat-trick of unsuccessful attempts.

Some of the original drawings I handed to Terry. Against my better judgement, there are a few more scattered through the pages of this book . . .

However, a few weeks later, once Terry had finished his signing tour, completely out of the blue, he rang me.

The upshot of our conversation (somewhat one-sided in Terry's favour with a rather speechless recipient) was an invitation to his Wiltshire home to discuss projects. It was a wintry afternoon in early 1994 when I drove to Broad Chalke to Terry's recently acquired stone manor house hidden in the Chalke valley of the River Ebble. By the woodburner in his office over the double garage I showed him my sketchbook filled with Discworld character designs. I asked permission to create a limited-edition print of The Librarian which Terry agreed to in return for a donation to the Orangutan Foundation. We also discussed calendars, further prints and an illustrated book of character drawings. When I left it was dark and for a few minutes we stood together marvelling at the Milky Way clearly visible over Cranborne Chase. A while later I heard that Victor Gollancz had agreed to the illustrated book; however, they were cautious about investing too heavily in an illustrator unknown to them and agreed to a modest paperback of 32 pages: The Pratchett Portfolio.

My Discworld journey had begun . . .

My original notebook sketch
for the Librarian print
and the finished piece

For twenty years I worked in collaboration with Terry, designing his world and visualizing his characters. For our first project, *The Pratchett Portfolio*, I would often visit Terry and we would discuss ideas for illustrations. Visiting the pathologically private author in his own home remained an exhilarating experience for me. Our common interests in art, history, popular culture, science, astronomy and nature gave us a broad base for inspiration; sometimes he would give me ideas and sometimes I would inspire him back. Despite Terry's growing stature in the fantasy world, our relationship was one of mutual respect: he didn't want adoration, but like me, wanted to get down to work.

When Terry so sadly passed away at the young age of 66, I felt he had prepared me well to continue holding a torch to light up the pictorial aspects of Discworld into the future. For the past decade I have continued to do this and have felt honoured to be able to be a part of his continuing legacy. Through my career as the Discworld artist, I have created the imagery for covers, maps, diaries, calendars and books and I now have a vast back catalogue of thirty years' worth of drawings and paintings and a head full of ideas still to visit. This book brings these things together in a celebration of illustrating Discworld and charts my journey and design process, discussing all manner of things from my preferred type of pencil to my penchant for dragons . . . and Nobby Nobbs.

Some of my early
projects with Terry

'These are good,' he said. 'What are they?'

'My cartoons,' said Leonard.

'This is a good one of the little boy with his kite stuck in a tree,' said Lord Vetinari.

MEN AT ARMS

ON PARODIES...

During the thirty years that I have been illustrating Terry Pratchett's Discworld, I have created many works that parody or pay homage to famous and much-loved paintings, photographs, films, television shows and album covers. These pieces intend respectfully to honour the original creators and to use their works as a starting point for my own interpretive Discworld twist. Hopefully, doing so brings an extra dimension of humour to my work.

I take an existing work of art as a basis for a new painting only if I consider it to be fitting to do so in every way. Terry's writing constantly references works of literature and film, with footnotes and parallels to the popular culture of 'Roundworld'. Adopting the same technique by visual means seems to complement this culturally eclectic approach.

My parody pieces are worked with one easel leg rooted in art history and the other firmly planted in Discworld, bridging a cultural divide between fantasy writing and the art world. Famously, Picasso stated, 'Good artists borrow, great artists steal.' I hope my viewers agree that I have successfully borrowed, if not stolen, to give my illustrations a personality of their own that is independent of their source material.

I have an impractically large collection of art reference books* and I browse through them often, making mental notes with magpie-like enthusiasm for the treasures they hold and the opportunities they offer for parody. Some of my paintings take very famous works as their starting point, such as the *Mona Ogg*, a grinning parody of the *Mona Lisa*. Others are more obscure and might, therefore, bring a sense of reward to the viewer who recognizes the source material I have taken inspiration from.

Not all my works pay tribute in the manner that Manet's *Olympia* honoured Titian's *Venus of Urbino*, but I hope that they raise a smile in the viewer – as they did for me when I painted them.

* I maintain that the book 'Extraordinary Chickens' is an invaluable addition to anyone's collection.

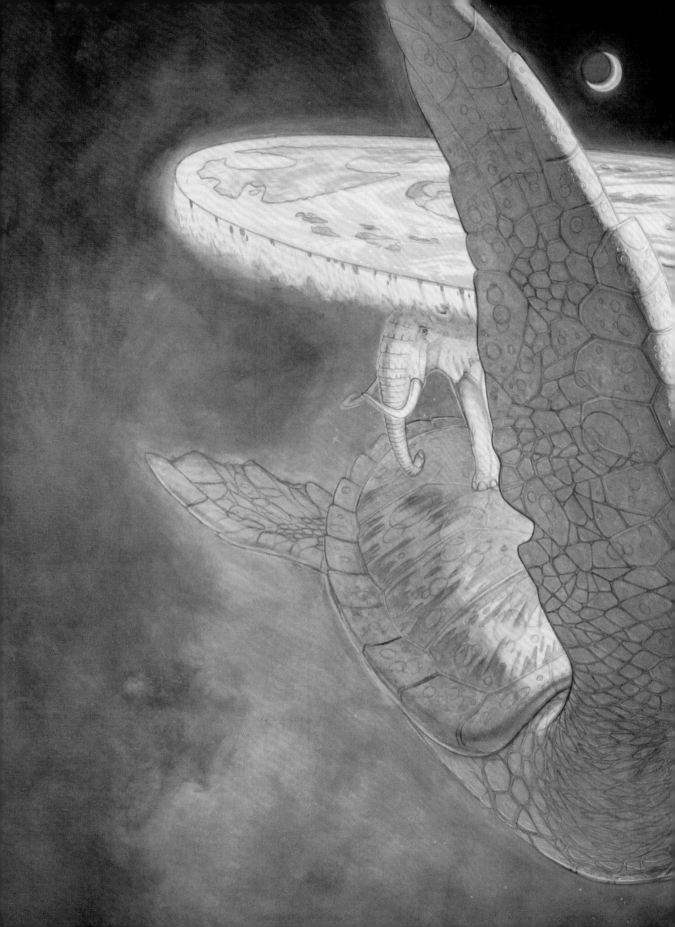

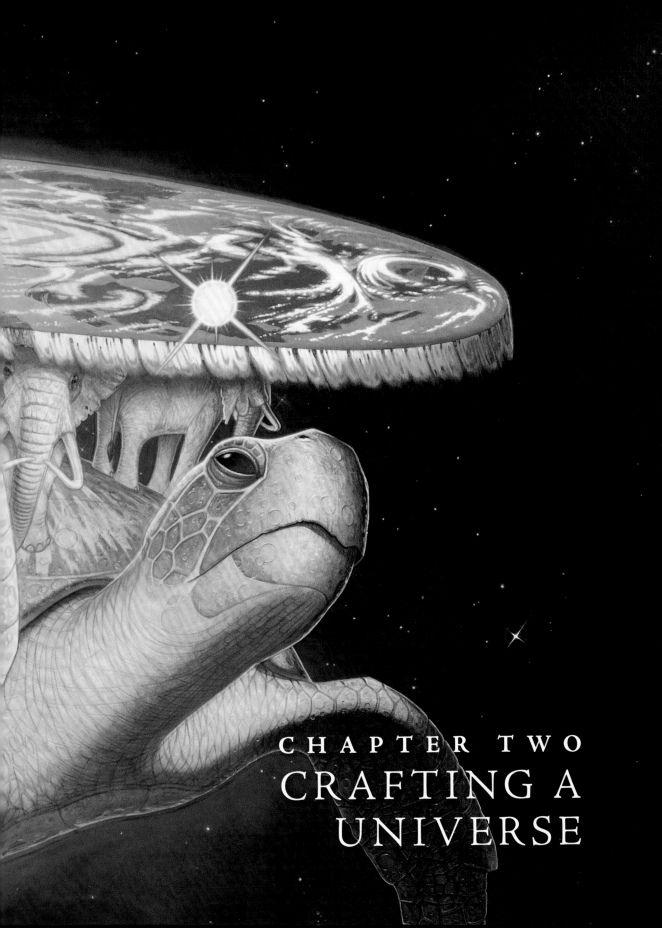

CHAPTER TWO
CRAFTING A UNIVERSE

Kachhapa, the world turtle as described in Hindu mythology

> *Where do you get your fantastic ideas from? You steal them. You steal them from reality. It outstrips fantasy most of the time.*
>
> TERRY PRATCHETT

IN THE BEGINNING...

Terry, to his polite chagrin, was most often asked two questions: Where did he get his ideas from? And how did he come up with Discworld, the world sat atop four elephants, themselves stood upon the shell of the vast star turtle, Great A'Tuin?

Terry would often quip that there was a little kiosk around the back of Basingstoke train station that sold good ideas, but would usually go on to explain that he found inspiration in the real world – Roundworld, to give it its Discworld moniker.

Terry had an appetite for the esoteric that only real life could match. He both read and collected books on a vast range of topics and was notorious for remembering obscure factoids people told him, which would often end up in his writing.

As for the idea of a world borne through space on a turtle, Terry would cheerfully tell anyone who asked that the idea had its roots in a number of mythologies, most notably Hindu.

Terry was also a proud, self-proclaimed member of what he called 'the school of recyclable literature'. No idea was too special to reuse; in fact his 1976 novel *The Dark Side of the Sun* introduced the concept of Hogswatch, while his 1981 novel *Strata* featured a flat planet – before the creation of Discworld.

People often ask artists which tools, which *particular* paints and brushes they use, in the hope of emulating their style, but focusing on the disparate elements of any creative process is rarely useful. Terry, like so many great creatives, knew it was the persistence and application of hard work that were key to creating something truly great.

My first painting of Great A'Tuin showed the light creeping slowly across the Disc, as Terry described. I set the second version in full sunlight to show the flatness of the whole disc . . .

GREAT A'TUIN
AND THE WORLD ELEPHANTS

hen Terry wrote *The Colour of Magic*, published in 1983, he was three novels into his writing career and still working at the South Western Region of the Central Electricity Generating Board. This book, however, marked a turning point – the beginning of Discworld. I didn't receive my paperback copy until ten years later, by which time Discworld was fourteen books in and had evolved into a genre all of its own. Terry's writing encompassed everything I loved: fantasy, bizarre humour, science fiction,

and an all-knowing eye when it came to the human condition, all set upon the back of the giant star turtle Great A'Tuin. The sex of whom is one of the great mysteries of Discworld.

Designing the Disc itself was an important early step of immersing myself in Terry's creation. I first painted Great A'Tuin for a Discworld Special edition of *SFX Magazine* in 1997. I based it on the Green Sea Turtle, which looked to me like the friendliest one in my bumper book of turtles. I also referenced images of the craters on the moon as inspiration for the meteor-pockmarked craters on its shell, face and body. I scratched into

Raw umber acrylic underpainting

Black base colour for space

Building up washes of colour

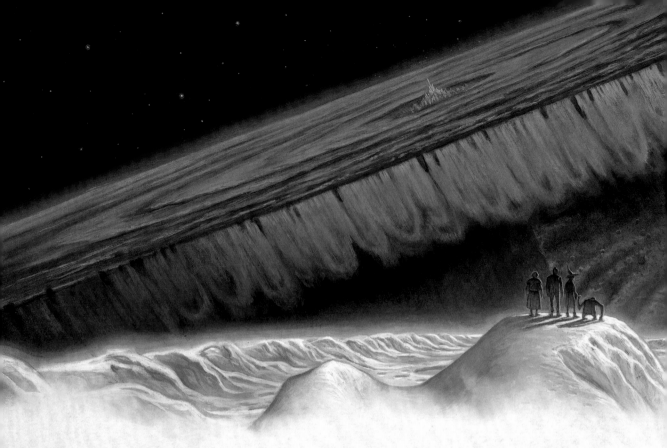

the surface of the oil paint with a scalpel to give texture and detail (which I later learned is an actual artistic technique called sgraffito, from the Italian for 'scratched').

The original painting was not done on a particularly large scale and so when I was commissioned by a private collector in 2012 to recreate it I did it much bigger, using acrylic on canvas. We hired a van to deliver it to Brussels, stopping in Bruges for a waffle on our way.

I have illustrated Great A'Tuin many times since my first version, in a number of styles. The turtle motif recurs throughout Discworld, appearing in many different magical and cultural contexts.

I think Terry got rather fed up with explaining the turtle in interviews. I hope the artwork makes the idea slightly quicker to digest.

The four elephants on whose backs the Disc rests are of the majestic African species because they are larger than their Indian cousins, and

Originally drawn for 'The Science of Discworld', this illuminated turtle design includes alchemical symbols for the four elements.

When painting Great T'Phon rising over the Discworld moon I chose a wide-angled composition to emphasize the astronomical scale of the subject matter.

have domed heads, big ears and long tusks. I love astronomy, nature and illustrating wildlife, so this commission of Great T'Phon, the world elephant, was a wonderful way to embrace Discworld whilst celebrating these amazing animals. The painting still hangs above the fireplace in Terry's writing room where he placed it.

'There was only one survivor, whose dying words were . . . rather strange.'

'I remember,' said Ridcully. 'He said, "My God, it's full of elephants!"'

THE LAST HERO

As the crew of the 'Kite' travel under the Disc in 'The Last Hero', Leonard makes sketches of the fabulous creatures they see on their journey including the astronomical-sized scarabs responsible for collecting the elephants' dung on the shell of Great A'Tuin, into which it lays eggs. As above, so below . . .

CHAPTER THREE
THE WIZARDS

RINCEWIND

Terry's first Discworld novel stars Rincewind, accidental hero, inept wizard and deliberate coward. Rincewind was the very first Discworld character I designed and he was amongst the drawings that I handed to Terry at the book signing all those years ago.

Although he has developed visually over the years, the original sketched DNA of this scared and scrawny wizard remains the same. His face is long, his hair is straggly and his physique is gangly (being very good at running away, he would, I imagined, have a level of athleticism unusual for a university academic). His robe and hat are embellished with stars and runes – sewn himself – and look appropriately amateurish. The belt around his middle accentuates his thin waist and his robes do not obscure his legs in order to show their extreme wiry build.

My very first ever Discworld drawings were these Rincewind designs which I gave to Terry.

Whilst I do not identify myself closely with Rincewind I think it is fair to say that some of my illustrations of him bear a resemblance to me – perhaps it's the inability to grow a proper beard or the slightly worried and world-weary expression. Despite Rincewind's reluctance he always seems to find himself at the centre of the action in a hero role, which is very endearing.

Rincewind has an uncanny habit of attracting tentacles.

Rincewind had been generally reckoned by his tutors to be a natural wizard in the same way that fish are natural mountaineers.

THE LIGHT FANTASTIC

My most recent drawing of
Rincewind as he appears
in 'The Colour of Magic'

DISCWORLD PARODY: THE SCREAM

Rincewind could scream for mercy in nineteen languages, and just scream in another forty-four.

INTERESTING
TIMES

his is a parody of Norwegian expressionist artist Edvard Munch's iconic *The Scream*, a powerful image which he created four times in various media in 1893. On one version Munch poignantly wrote in pencil, 'could only have been painted by a madman'.

Munch used colour to portray emotion: in this case the red-streaked sky indicates the anxiety and dis-ease of the subject.

The image has become embedded in popular culture, representing fear and anxiety, so therefore the scenario described in *The Last Hero* of a terrified Rincewind on the moon being confronted with the vast elephant Great T'Phon seemed to lend itself to a parody of the work. Where the two figures are positioned in the original I have included the other crew of the *Kite*: Carrot, Leonard and the Librarian, all of whom look less concerned.

This painting was commissioned for a new, expanded paperback edition of *The Last Hero* – Terry felt the book deserved an encore, in the form of some additional art, when it came to be released in a new format.

Rincewind crops up plenty more times in the Discworld series – usually against his will, I suspect – because fans so frequently asked Terry when he would next appear.

One of my favourite Rincewind pieces is my painting of Rincewind and Conina. This painting was inspired by *Conan the Adventurer*, by American fantasy and comic-book artist Frank Frazetta. The original version features the chauvinistic male hero with a trophy damsel-in-distress clinging to his leg in an iconic fantasy pose. My version, in the interest of parity, depicts Conina in the hero stance with Rincewind clinging to her leg. Terry's writing often turns the tables on gender bias, and it is only right that I do the same with my artwork. Frank passed away while I was working on this piece, and so my painting became not only a tribute but also a memorial to him.

A sketch for a woodcut-style 'The Colour of Magic' cover. Rincewind's beard and hangdog expression make him recognizable in pretty much any style.

Terry's sketch of Rincewind, drawn for Bernard Pearson, which I only saw years later.
Rather pleasingly, you can see the line of descent from Terry's words, to his sketch, to my eventual artwork.

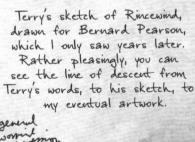

general worried expression

← Poor, shaggly beard

← 'ill-fitting robe

Rincewind

DISCWORLD PARODY: THE VITRUVIAN MAN

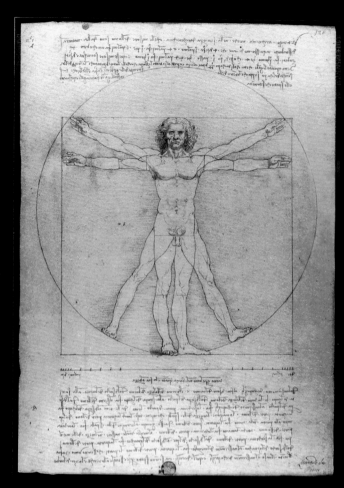

Initially, I drew Rincewind clothed in his robes, but it did not look right, so I redrew him in just a bincloth - far more effective and amusing.

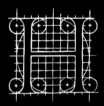

ere I set a nauseous Rincewind in the position of Leonardo's *Vitruvian Man*, which is a study of proportion by the great master, blending mathematics and art. The original was itself inspired by the Roman author and architect Vitruvius. It was Terry who suggested this parody, as he wanted to create a spread in *The Last Hero* that appeared to be the work of Leonard of Quirm, who is based on Leonardo da Vinci.

Leonardo is fun to parody on a number of levels – as an eccentric polymath genius he feels like a fantastical character even before he's been translated through the lens of Discworld. Besides drawing blueprints for inventions such as the aerial screw, a robotic knight and an armoured car, he dissected more than thirty corpses in his grisly quest to understand human anatomy.

My illustration is a study of the circulation of vomit and – as anyone who has been on the cage ride at the fair after a few shandies and a toffee apple will testify – it does indeed circulate.

Testing the Handiwork of the Gods

It being apparent that a voyage into the Great Void will result in much stress upon the human frame, I have devised this device of three rings that rotate continuously in three planes, giving the Voyager the feeling of being rotated continuously in three planes. It is vital to know if the human body, or at least that of the wizard Rincewind, can withstand such treatment.

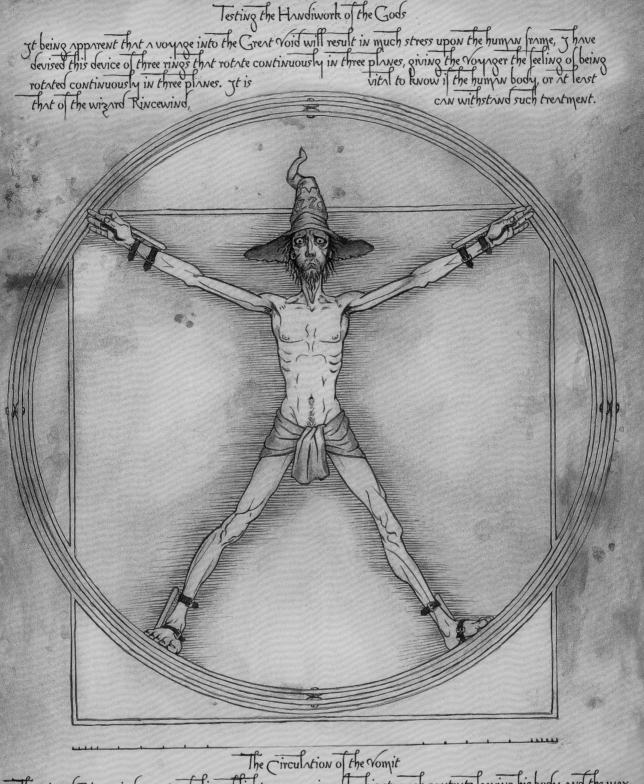

The Circulation of the Vomit

The wizard Rincewind reports a feeling of lightness occasioned by his stomach contents leaving his body and the wax running out of his ears. Prolonged tumbling on the device causes him to experience the feeling of wishing to kill everyone beginning, against all common sense, with himself. He also issues screams and threats. From this I deduce that being tumbled in three directions at once has a deleterious effect and I will arrange for this not to happen on the voyage. The musculature of the wizard Rincewind would make an interesting study if, indeed, he had any.

Leonard of
Quirm

DISCWORLD PARODY: APOLLO 11

'It will certainly be a challenge to go where no one has gone before,' said Carrot.

'Wrong! We're going where no one has come back from before.'
[Replied Rincewind]

THE LAST HERO

ne of my earliest memories is watching the Apollo moon landing with my family in 1969. In *The Last Hero* the crew of the *Kite* – Carrot, Leonard and the reluctant Rincewind – are sent on a space mission by Lord Vetinari. I felt that a parody of the classic photo of the astronauts Armstrong, Collins and Aldrin would be an appropriate illustration. In the original, the sitters look brave and confident; in my version, Rincewind looks decidedly nervous.

A mission patch featuring the motto 'Morituri nolumus mori' - 'We who are about to die, don't want to'. This is a play on the greeting from the gladiators to the Roman emperor, 'Morituri te salutant', 'Those who are about to die salute you'.

THE LUGGAGE

Terry ascribed a few different origins to the Luggage, claiming to have been inspired watching a wheeled suitcase bouncing after its owner on a cobbled street in Bath, whilst also mentioning his invention of an ill-behaved travelling storage chest during his time playing Dungeons and Dragons™.

Part of my design for the Luggage has always been its wide, toothy grin to convey its happy nature. The grain of the wood subtly suggests eyes. In recent years I've given it more uneven teeth, and more nicks and scratches. Illustrating an object shouldn't be this much fun, but it's testament to the strength of Terry's writing that it is.

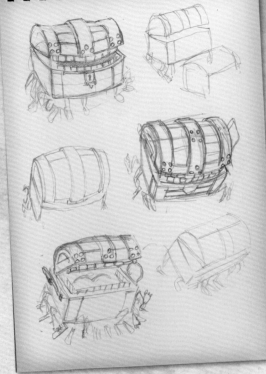

Early concept sketches. There are more poses than you might imagine for a wooden chest with legs.

It is described in Terry's writing as having hundreds of little legs. My depiction has fewer legs; during the design process I found that larger legs and feet seemed (bizarrely) more physically threatening.

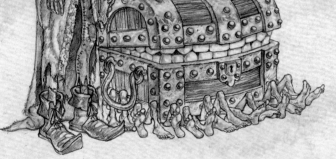

Why it consented to be owned by Rincewind was something only the Luggage knew, and it wasn't telling, but probably no other item in the entire chronicle of travel accessories had quite such a history of mystery and grievous bodily harm. It had been described as half suitcase, half homicidal maniac.

SOURCERY

THE LIBRARIAN

I first designed the Librarian in 1994. I had to endow this 300lb orangutan with a look of bookish intelligence. 'Orangutan' means 'man of the forest' and in Discworld this transformed wizard is a 'man of the library', using his long, powerful arms and grasping hands and feet to navigate the shelves of the multi-dimensional Unseen University Library. I didn't give my design the prominent cheekpads of dominant males as he has a quiet and scholarly demeanour;* instead I drew him with a large primitive brow, which is reflected in my portrait of Horace Worblehat before the magical accident in *The Light Fantastic* which transformed him. The two depictions also share the same facial hair pattern.

* It's also well established that Ridcully, not the Librarian, is the dominant male at Unseen University.

There was always this trouble with the Librarian. Everyone had got so accustomed to him it was hard to remember a time when the Library was not run by a yellow-fanged ape with the strength of three men.

MOVING PICTURES

 ne of the TV shows that Terry and I both enjoyed was *Monty Python's Flying Circus*, with its surreal comedy. In fact, I still have a much-treasured tin of Spam that Terry Jones signed for me.

The show's recurring character the nude organist inspired my painting of the Librarian playing the organ and the title is a hint at the source material. He has a broad smile, though Terry, who met real male orangutans in the wilds of Borneo, points out in *The Art of Discworld* that 'laughing or exposing your teeth in any way is not a sensible thing to do'.

The absurdist humour of Monty Python is perhaps to British humour what Tolkien is to fantasy – not so much an influence, as baked into the DNA. Terry always said that J. R. R. Tolkien had become a 'mountain': referencing him – or choosing not to – is a deliberate choice for fantasy authors. It's the same with Monty Python. Peter Jackson found this to his detriment when filming *The Lord of the Rings* – too often, the most prosaic fantasy elements would evoke scenes from *Monty Python and the Holy Grail*. Luckily, in the world of Discworld, and my own work, this influence is very welcome.

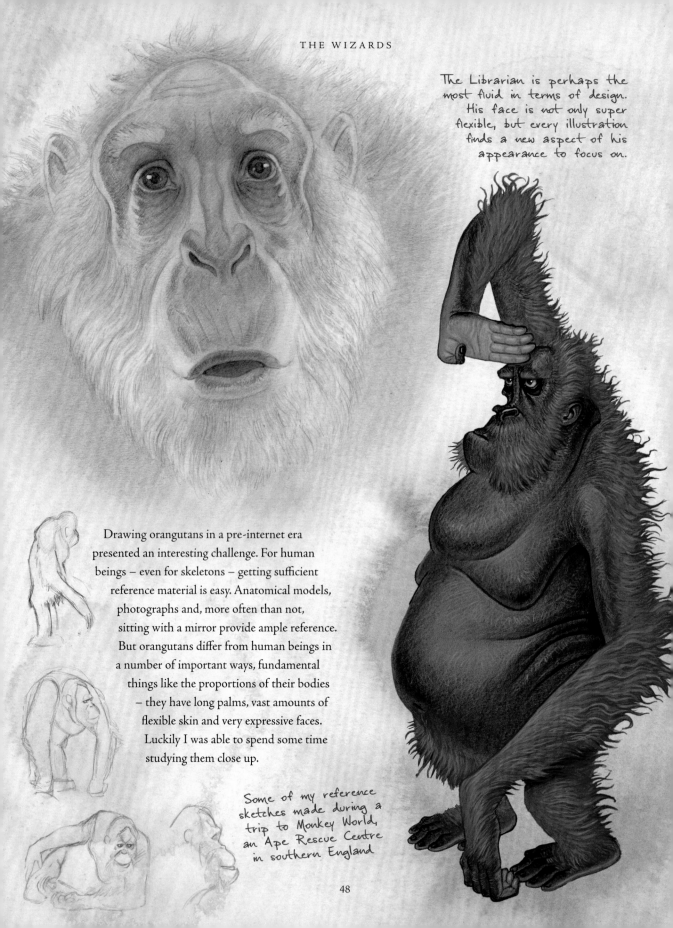

The Librarian is perhaps the most fluid in terms of design. His face is not only super flexible, but every illustration finds a new aspect of his appearance to focus on.

Drawing orangutans in a pre-internet era presented an interesting challenge. For human beings – even for skeletons – getting sufficient reference material is easy. Anatomical models, photographs and, more often than not, sitting with a mirror provide ample reference. But orangutans differ from human beings in a number of important ways, fundamental things like the proportions of their bodies – they have long palms, vast amounts of flexible skin and very expressive faces. Luckily I was able to spend some time studying them close up.

Some of my reference sketches made during a trip to Monkey World, an Ape Rescue Centre in southern England

48

Terry describes the Librarian as having fangs, but this is one of those rare times I've deviated from the source text – my depictions of him give him rather more human teeth, the better to provide a friendly smile. He retains all the other orangutanesque features though: Terry felt such long-limbed creatures were uniquely suited to work in libraries.

An early sketch showing the Librarian saying the less-uttered 'Eek'

The Librarian's City Watch badge, assigned to him in 'Guards! Guards!'. I chose 345, the Dewey decimal prefix for criminal law.

You didn't get anywhere at Unseen University without being able to understand the vast number of meanings that can be carried by the word 'ook'.

UNSEEN ACADEMICALS

 erry loved to bring classic film references into his novels and *Moving Pictures* is a great case in point with clear allusions to *King Kong*, made in 1933, which is still ranked as the greatest horror film of all time.

I painted the scene where, in typical Pratchett role reversal, Terry described a creature from the Dungeon Dimensions, in the form of a fifty-foot-tall Ginger, climbing the Tower of Art whilst holding the diminutive Librarian in its hand.

Looking back at the original movie I realize that the film-makers cleverly avoided this actual shot which would have been very complicated and expensive to create in the pre-digital era. They showed us instead the reactions of the people on the ground and relied on the viewers to use their imaginations.

'A giant woman carrying a screaming ape up a tall building,' sighed Dibbler. 'And we're not even having to pay wages!'

MOVING PICTURES

THE WIZARDS OF
UNSEEN UNIVERSITY

 I illustrate the wizards of Unseen University wearing Tudoresque garments: ecclesiastical-style robes, doublet and hose and a fancy line in pantaloons. These flamboyant outfits are festooned with eight-pointed stars,* mystical runes and mayoral-type chains that show off their owners' pomp and wealth. They are topped off with pointed hats.

My designs stem from a key description in *Equal Rites*:

> There were fashions in wizardry, just like anything else; sometimes wizards were thin and gaunt and talked to animals (the animals didn't listen, but it's the thought that counts) while at other times they tended towards the dark and saturnine, with little black pointed beards. Currently Aldermanic was In.

This tells us that the wizards were fashion-focused with a current tendency to show their rank through their choice of attire.

I never think of my work as 'definitive', as there's always room for improvement, but Terry did once confide in me that the makers of a Discworld TV adaptation depicting the wizards emphatically insisted they *weren't* referencing my work, yet seemed happy to stick every page of *The Art of Discworld* up on the walls of the production design office. C'est la vie!

Illustrations of Cutangle. My pencil drawing is the more recent, where he has broader shoulders (thanks to his outfit) and more of an authoritative air. His staff is also more ornate and unusual.

*Eight is a magic number and the wizards of Discworld use octograms instead of Roundworld's traditional esoteric pentangle.

THE TOWER OF ART

 hen designing this building, my first attempts were fairly standard fantasy edifices. My very first illustration borrows perhaps more from Disney than I'd like now, but subsequent attempts took on board more architectural reference and I pushed the organic elements further.

For the most recent iteration, I looked at the painting by Pieter Bruegel the Elder of *The Tower of Babel* (1563) and gave my illustration a similar architectural structure with numerous arches reminiscent of the Roman Colosseum. I drew the natural rock as a strong, broad foundation that tapers upwards to a great height; a small door at the base leads to a spiral staircase. I wanted the tower to look as if the ancient geology of the Disc has been pulled and spun skywards (800 feet), into a marvel of engineering, as old and mysterious as the Discworld itself. Its appearance is largely organic and natural as if the architectural additions of crenellations and turrets are wizardly afterthoughts.

First and second development sketches for the Tower of Art

DISCWORLD PARODY: AN EXPERIMENT ON A BIRD IN THE AIR PUMP

Joseph Wright of Derby is most known for his work done during the 'age of enlightenment' in the late 1700s. His paintings show the conflict at the time between burgeoning science and religion. His dramatic use of lighting with large areas of black paint is known as tenebrism, which is an extreme version of chiaroscuro; both are Italian terms for theatrical illumination.

My painting takes inspiration from one of two candlelight paintings by Wright depicting scientific experiments. In *An Experiment on a Bird in the Air Pump* a vacuum is being created within the jar to see what will happen to the unlucky cockatoo inside it. The atmospheric painting reminded me of the environment of Unseen University and the

wizards of Discworld. In my version, Roundworld is within the bell jar rather than the bird, which is not part of the experiment and is watching the procedure from the safety of its cage. The Dean in the background is holding a squash racket over his shoulder and looks disgruntled: this is because the squash court in Unseen University has been converted into the High Energy Magic Building. The Roundworld parallel to this was the nuclear research done in a converted squash court in the University of Chicago in 1942, which led to the Manhattan Project.

Terry owned my original painting, which was one of his favourites; in fact he maintained that if his office caught fire, it would be the one artefact he'd tuck under his arm before running out of the door.

I had been waiting to parody Joseph Wright of Derby, and when Terry asked me to create the cover for 'The Science of Discworld', it seemed the perfect fit.

'I really think it might be a good *idea* if they stopped playing squash, sir,' he whispered.

'Me too. There's nothing worse than a sweaty wizard. Stop it, you fellows. And gather round. Mr Stibbons is going to do his presentation.'

THE SCIENCE OF DISCWORLD

RIDCULLY

This character is big and loud and in robust health. He has a passion for hunting, shooting and fishing and is more often found out in the grounds than seated in the offices of Unseen University academia. I depicted him with a large bristly beard to indicate vast amounts of testosterone, and a high ruddy colouring. His wizard's robes are made of hardwearing brown leather more suited for the outdoors, with big practical pockets. His hat is notorious for its handy drawers and the band is festooned with his fishing flies. The top of the hat unscrews to make a cup for a tipple.

'Art's for slackers!'

THE SCIENCE OF
DISCWORLD II

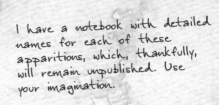

In *Reaper Man* Ridcully's curses take on a life of their own. It was a lot of fun designing the visual look of each swear word. Terry described these 'expletives' as insect-like with wings, multiple eyes and stings. The one with horrible eyebrows is clearly a *very* bad word.

I have a notebook with detailed names for each of these apparitions, which, thankfully, will remain unpublished. Use your imagination.

Ridcully is sometimes styled as 'Ridcully the Brown', in a possible nod to Tolkien's nature-loving wizard Radagast the Brown. Alas, Ridcully's interest in the natural world is more focused towards hunting, eating and stuffing its inhabitants. Perhaps one exception is the Librarian, whom Ridcully is content to simply arm-wrestle. As already noted, the Librarian lacks the cheek pouches of dominant adult orangutans due to the fact that Ridcully is the alpha male at Unseen University.

Having spent almost all my adult life in the countryside I am very familiar with this type of person who has to be reminded to use their indoor voice.

Hughnon Ridcully, Mustrum's brother, is High Priest of Blind Io, and a slightly less bombastic character than his brother. Still, you can see a similar familial look of stubbornness in his expression.

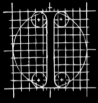 painted this for the 2011 Discworld calendar, to tie in with Terry's 37th Discworld novel, *Unseen Academicals*, a story that focuses on football at Unseen University. It seemed only fitting that I take my visual starting point from the classic photograph of England Captain Bobby Moore being carried by his teammates after lifting the World Cup in 1966.

The title comes from Kenneth Wolstenholme's legendary commentary, 'They think it's all over; it is now!'

I really don't know much about football other than a vague notion of running, shouting and mud, and I think it would be fair to say that Terry didn't either! For him it conjured a world of pies, chants and jumpers for goalposts.

Of all the characters in the painting, I identify most with Rincewind (I usually do), who looks like he'd rather be anywhere else in the world, except perhaps playing rugby.

'You see, the thing about football is
that it is not about football.'

UNSEEN ACADEMICALS

When I was painting this cover for 'Unseen Academicals', I pitched creating it in sepia tones to hark back to historical team photos. However, the publishers requested I take it to full colour. It was amusing therefore to see the final book jacket had been digitally altered back to sepia!

UNSEEN ACADEMICALS

RIDCULLY

LIBRARIAN

NUTT

RINCEWIND

HIX

To celebrate the publication of *Unseen Academicals*, Terry commissioned me to paint a series of football cards. He, like me, had always been a fan of the collectable cards issued in Brooke Bond packs of tea and this seemed a perfect opportunity to create a Discworld equivalent. The full set comprised a number of players mentioned in the novel, but also featured longtime Terry collaborator Bernard Pearson and myself as unlikely substitutes and is probably the closest I've come to caricature-style artwork.

CHARLIE

PONDER STIBBONS

ALF NOBBS
(NO RELATION)

TREVOR LIKELY

BENGO MACARONA

ANKH-MORPORK UNITED

CHARLIE (BIG BOY)
BARTON

DAVID (DAVE) LIKELY

THE ARCHCHANCELLOR
FORMERLY KNOWN AS
THE DEAN

ANDY SHANK

J.W. RICKETT

JIMMY WILKINS

JOSEPH HOGGETT

AKNON SMYTH

BERNARD
(THE BOLT)
PEARSON

PAUL
(THE OTHER ONE)
KIDBY

GRYFFID
TABERNACLE
EVANS

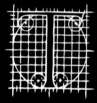his is a Discworldian take on another of Joseph Wright of Derby's candlelight pictures titled *A Philosopher giving that Lecture on the Orrery, in which a lamp is put in the place of the Sun*. Like Leonard of Quirm, Derby wasn't averse to a rather verbose title.

The painting is similar to the Air Pump work where the artist is depicting a demonstration of the wonders of the universe to onlookers at a time of scientific discovery.

In my version the Unseen University faculty are discussing the flight path of the *Kite* spaceship with Vetinari. A tracery of lines depicts the magical orrery, each colour representing a different element: Great A'Tuin is green, the

Disc blue, the sun's orbit orange, the moon's orbit purple and red displays the flight of the *Kite*.

In parodying a piece like this, the composition and lighting are already set and matching them is relatively simple. The challenge is in choosing the right characters to go in the right places whilst also making sure they are depicted in a style that's still recognizable.

Both Terry and I enjoyed astronomy and around the time of creating this painting we spent time observing the rings of Saturn together in his brand-new observatory.

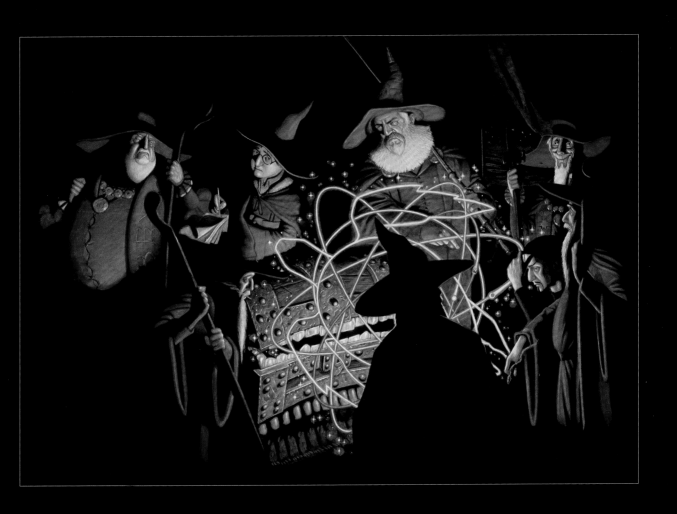

*Lord Vetinari looked at the big spell that
dominated the cabin. It floated in the air:
the whole world, sketched in glowing lines
and, dropping from one glittering edge,
a small curving line.*

THE LAST HERO

MYRIAD OTHER WIZARDS

I am generally my own fiercest critic, which is how it should be. Very occasionally I feel fully pleased and this painting of Eric was one of those occasions where my character design seemed to capture all the nerdy physiology of this (nearly) fourteen-year-old self-styled demonologist.

Coin, the eighth son of an eighth son and therefore a sourcerer, needed to look sinister and powerful. He has strange glowing eyes and a possessed staff which carries his father's controlling spirit. The emblem on his cloak fastening is an ancient Viking symbol that consists of three overlapping and interconnected arcs; it represents father and son. This is fitting for Coin.

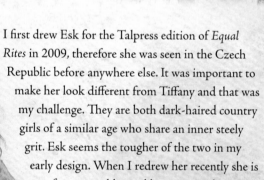

I first drew Esk for the Talpress edition of *Equal Rites* in 2009, therefore she was seen in the Czech Republic before anywhere else. It was important to make her look different from Tiffany and that was my challenge. They are both dark-haired country girls of a similar age who share an inner steely grit. Esk seems the tougher of the two in my early design. When I redrew her recently she is a few years older and has more wide-set eyes with a clear-viewed expression that looks less disgruntled. In this second drawing she has accepted her fate as a wizard and grown into her power. The tall wizard's staff, which is initially disguised as a broomstick, is intricately carved in organic shapes.

Drum Billet, a wizard's wizard. He fits all the standard fantasy archetypes, from the big white beard to the staff. One of the runes on his robes represents an ant: a clue to his eventual fate.

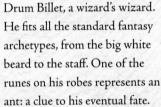

Simon is an academic wizard. In this portrait, he has a gentle, bemused expression and holds a book of magic with an octogram design. His lack of presence belies his great potential. I warm to his personality and I think that shows in my drawing.

Brian strikes me as potentially pompous and is what I would describe as a jobbing wizard. My drawing gives him an air of disdain, even as a frog.

I designed the ruler of Krull with an ancient Mesopotamian-influenced outfit. He sports a carefully tended beard as was the fashion in Assyria and Babylonia, which I think of as historical real-world parallels to Krull. He wears a clearly high-status hat embroidered with male and female symbols to signify the big question – the gender of Great A'Tuin. His pendant is an astrolabe.

Terry describes Krull's fifth-level female wizard Marchesa as having black skin and white hair. I gave her bantu knots as a symbol of pride and self-expression. She carries Ajandurah's Wand of Utter Negativity. The brooch on her robes bears a Krullian design: the star turtle surrounded by stars, reflecting Krull's prowess in astronomy.

CHAPTER FOUR
THE WITCHES

GRANNY WEATHERWAX

Terry based Granny Weatherwax on lots of old ladies, including his own grandmother, and then multiplied everything by ten. She didn't necessarily soften as the books progressed, but she definitely found new depths.

Granny's expression has always been loosely based on my mother, who came from a farm in mid Wales where the landscape is not dissimilar to Lancre, and who, like Granny, was as stern as slate. I first drew her in 1993 as part of my pitching package for Terry. I then refined the character design for *The Pratchett Portfolio*, bringing in the descriptive elements from the text such as her hobnailed boots, moon brooch and crocheted black shawl.

I have drawn Granny at various stages through her life. Terry liked my first version of young Esme so much that he bought the original. I revisited this depiction in 2022 for *The Ultimate Discworld Companion*. This later version is less of a caricature: although youthful she still has the severely tied-back hair, direct stare, arched brow and unsmiling mouth as the portraits of Granny in later life. It shows that her single-minded, no-nonsense personality was formed at an early age and she was never one to be easily swayed by the fripperies of fashion. As part of the depiction of her buttoned-up personality I always give Granny a high-necked collar.

Paul's depiction of Granny Weatherwax is, to me, exactly, shockingly right; his rendition of Granny as a girl astonished me, because it was so clearly her, you could see her future in her eyes.

TERRY PRATCHETT

Witches are not by nature gregarious, [. . .] and they certainly don't have leaders. Granny Weatherwax was the most highly regarded of the leaders they didn't have.

WYRD SISTERS

Granny's broomstick* riding position: upright, disapproving and side-saddle

*'Borrowed' from Hilta Goatfounder

NANNY OGG

Everybody's favourite Nanny: most of us have met her big-hearted type at one time or another. When I draw Gytha I try to capture a joyful and raucous love of life in her expression. Her lack of worry and eagerness to embrace all good things define her personality. Her stature is small and round and her face is wrinkled and split with a wide toothless smile. She makes a great counterfoil in both stature and personality to Granny Weatherwax and I have drawn them together many times.

I depict Nanny in a simple low-cut dress ('off the shoulder and on to the grass' as Granny acerbically observes). Her chosen footwear is heeled red boots complemented by striped red stockings. Her usual accessories are a small clay pipe with a bowl fashioned like a hedgehog, a tankard and of course her cat Greebo.

Nanny's cottage is neat and tidy thanks to her numerous daughters-in-law. It has fresh thatch and a garden full of flowers, gnomes, and other garden ornaments.
My own parents had a windmill by their pond, which makes me feel a bit nostalgic.

I had particular fun illustrating *Nanny Ogg's Cookbook*, despite working on several other projects at the same time. Terry specifically requested that Nanny Ogg be wielding a courgette and a knife on the front cover.* Working with Terry on diaries and companion books was one of my very favourite parts of illustrating Discworld. All the unusual asides and jokes which are scattered through the novels are densely packed in these sorts of project and gave me the chance to illustrate some of the most esoteric subjects.

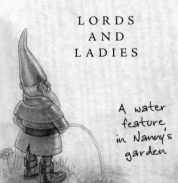

Nanny and Greebo drawn for the author picture in 'Nanny Ogg's Cookbook': this image parodies the image of Delia Smith with her cat in 'How to Cook: vol 1'.

*I also included nettles, as Terry liked to remind me that this was the perfect food for impoverished artists. He even gave me his recipe for nettle soup.

She was an incredibly comfortable person to be around, partly because she had a mind so broad it could accommodate three football fields and a bowling alley.

LORDS
AND
LADIES

A water feature, in Nanny's garden

Another illustration from the cookbook – a fun piece of visual storytelling.

FLOUR

DISCWORLD PARODY: THE MONA LISA

'The teeth followed you around the room. Amazing. In fact some people said they followed them out of the room and all the way down the street.'

MEN AT ARMS

I also wanted to create a version with the contemporary Nanny Ogg (and Greebo) that readers are familiar with.

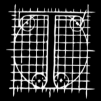he temptation to parody the most famous painting in the world, the *Mona Lisa*, also called *Portrait of Lisa Gherardini, wife of Francesco del Giocondo*, was too much to ignore. In my version, I have imagined a young Gytha Ogg as the artist Leonard of Quirm's muse, complete with her extremely un-enigmatic smile. This is my second version of Mona Ogg (the first was on the cover of *The Art of Discworld*, published in 2004). I came back to it because I felt I could do it better and portray Gytha as more comely. I also wanted to include a disapproving Esme Weatherwax in the background and two carved hedgehogs on the balustrade as a reference to Gytha's song of preference. I offer this with sincere apologies to Leonardo da Vinci.

Leonard of Quirm

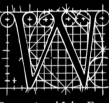 illiam Holman Hunt was in 1848 a founder member of the Pre-Raphaelite Brotherhood, along with Dante Gabriel Rossetti and John Everett Millais. This group of young men in their early twenties were fed up with the ethos of the Royal Academy of Art and its president Sir Joshua Reynolds, who they called Sir Sloshua. They set out to follow the art style of the early Italian Renaissance: the era preceding the time of Raphael. This art was colourful, detailed and true to nature, often with a moral theme. It's hard to believe nowadays that their work caused an outraged public reaction to their naturalistic portrayal of religious themes. Dickens himself declared that Millais had made the Holy Family look like alcoholics and slum-dwellers. I personally greatly admire their precise work and visual storytelling which is often loaded with symbolism and pictorial clues.

William Holman Hunt painted *The Hireling Shepherd* in 1851. I have long admired this painting and am amused by the *Athenaeum* magazine review that was particularly offended by these 'rustics of the coarsest breed . . . flushed and rubicund' from too much cider. My version transports the bucolic scene to Lancre and features a young Gytha Ogg with an amorous Leonard of Quirm. In the original, the shepherd is neglecting his flock, while in my version the young Leonard is distracted from his drawings by his alluring companion. I included a hedgehog in her lap as a reminder of her favourite song. The apples are a reference to her legendary Scumble Cider. When I showed my drawing to Terry in 2003, he requested that I add a model of an aerial screw in Leonard's hand. I have included within this painting a secondary parody. One of Leonard's sketches that are being blown in the wind is of a nude Gytha Ogg; the pose is taken from the film *Titanic* when Jack draws Rose 'like one of your French girls'.

'You always used to say I was wanton, when we
was younger,' said Nanny.

'You was, of course,' [Granny] said dismissively.
'But you never used magic for it, did you?'

'Din't have to,' said Nanny happily. 'An off-the-shoulder
dress did the trick most of the time.'

'Right off the shoulder and on to the grass,
as I recall,' said Granny.

WITCHES ABROAD

iego Velázquez was born in Seville, Spain in 1599 and became a royal portraitist and leading artist of the Spanish Golden Age. He was inspired by classical antiquity on his travels in Italy which led him to paint *The Toilet of Venus*, also known as 'The Rokeby Venus' after the grand house Rokeby Park in County Durham, where it hung in Victorian times.

Most of the artist's work remained in the private collections of Spanish royalty until the turbulence of the Peninsular War when Napoleon invaded Spain. During this time the paintings were seized from the palaces and became scattered through Europe.

Velázquez is famous for his ability to capture form and light, and his dexterous handling of paint; to this day he is known as the painter's

painter (as Manet termed him). There are fewer than 150 signed works extant, and *Venus* is his only surviving female nude.

I also appreciate the fact that he is known to have worked slowly, which I can identify with. As a footnote in *A Life with Footnotes* by Rob Wilkins observes: 'This might be a good moment to mention that the logo for Paul's business was two snails facing each other, or to use the correct armorial term, two snails rampant'.

I can imagine that in her youth Nanny Ogg took delight in being a nearly naked (and a completely naked) muse to lots of different artists – and this parody is just one of many that I hold in my head.

My version has a disapproving young Esme Weatherwax lurking behind the urn.

An early sketch of Greebo

GREEBO

Greebo radiated genuine intelligence. He also radiated a smell that would have knocked over a wall and caused sinus trouble in a dead fox.

WYRD SISTERS

Trying to make a cat look like it would win a fight with a bear was my challenge when designing Greebo. His confident swagger and malevolent expression were important to capture. This was done by using direct eye contact (just the one) and making the composition from a mouse-eye view. This means using a low-angle perspective to make him seem more formidable. Giving him many scars and bits missing from his ears helps to reinforce his battle history.

I have drawn Greebo a number of times over the years but as far as I am concerned this is the definitive version. Fleabitten, scarred, blind in one eye, with ragged ears, he is an enormous bully of a cat – renowned for once chasing a wolf up a tree. This is the cat that Nanny Ogg refers to as 'a big old softie' and sees, in her head, as a cute little bundle of fluff.

78

When designing Greebo in his transformation to human shape, I was thinking along the lines of a young Sean Bean as he appeared in *Sharpe* (before his days as Boromir or Ned Stark), handsome with an edge of danger. I tried to imbue him with smouldering sex appeal which is helped along by his unbuttoned shirt, hairy chest and confident posture that conveys feline allure.

Memories of Genua

I ensured there was a similarity in Greebo's profile whether as a cat or a man. Both have the same slant of the eye and a feline smile.

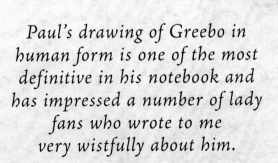

Paul's drawing of Greebo in human form is one of the most definitive in his notebook and has impressed a number of lady fans who wrote to me very wistfully about him.

TERRY PRATCHETT

MAGRAT

Magrat has the look of a New Age witch complete with lots of occult jewellery, crystals and dangly earrings. Having lived many years in the West Country I am very familiar with her type. Magrat has a timid personality, with watery eyes and a red nose from frequent upsets. Over the course of her story arc, she becomes more confident and assertive as she finds her place in life. Most of my illustrations are of her at the beginning of her journey where she looks more worried and uncertain.

I drew this armoured Magrat many years ago, always intending that, in colour, she'd be splattered with blood, a detail which adds a certain something . . .

Magrat in armour is an illustration from *Lords and Ladies* where, over her wedding dress, she puts on the protective battle armour of Queen Ynci, a mythical Boudica-type warrior queen. The winged helmet and breastplate awake within her a warlike spirit despite them being nothing more than a costume, and a rather too-big one at that. My drawing is based on Celtic armour complete with spikes and a winged helmet. The image is a gentle poke at the traditional comic-book female warrior figure, as Magrat is clearly not cut out for the wearing of such garb or the wielding of giant double-headed axes.

THE KINGDOM OF
LANCRE

My illustration depicts the castle from a bird's-eye view to include the steep cliffs and ravines it perches above. I took inspiration from the Gothic Revival Lichtenstein Castle in Germany, which is built in a fairytale style and, like Lancre, sited atop a rocky outcrop high above a river. My drawing shows a crenellated medieval gateway, the crumbled remains of outer curtain walls and round corner towers that have mostly fallen into the gorges below. The interior buildings are an architectural mixture spanning the centuries and include a Norman-style keep with observation turrets, timber-framed domestic buildings and stone halls. The steep-pitched tower roofs are influenced by the French castle of Carcassonne. I also included dangerous stairways that end abruptly above perilous drops and bridges spanning chasms in the rock to accentuate the precarious nature of this castle.

If you look very closely you can see Hodgesaargh being chased by his falcons and Shawn Ogg asleep at the bottom of the gate tower.

WITCHES APLENTY

Dilith, sister to Esme Weatherwax – like so often in Terry's writing the visually attractive character hides unpleasantness within. The design challenge is to convey the sinister heart that lies behind the charming exterior. Anatomically, she is identical to Granny Weatherwax, but pose, lighting and colour go a long way towards differentiating the two.

Nothing stood in the way of what Lilith liked more than anything else.

A happy ending.

WITCHES ABROAD

Miss Tick. In my latest depiction I thought it fitting to draw her with a resemblance to Indira Varma, who has narrated the new Penguin Audio editions of the Tiffany Aching series.

A previous design for Miss Tick (left). Sometimes inspiration hits, even if I've only recently illustrated a character.

Miss Level – Terry requested that I draw her with a likeness to Margaret Rutherford, who starred in classic films of the post-war era. I have always kept to his direction.

It's perhaps only when I see some of them here that I realize how many Discworld witches I've illustrated and how varied Terry made them.

Hilta Goatfounder. My first design of her shows her love of colour and abundant ethnic jewellery. She is warm-hearted and, I imagine, scented with patchouli oil.

In my second version I realized there was room for even more jewellery and beads. I love reiterating a design, it's like bringing a person into focus.

Geoffrey, a male witch and calm-weaver. As a vegetarian pacifist I relate to this chap so he has a certain visual likeness to myself as a young man. He has inherited Granny's broomstick which she had in turn 'borrowed' – thus the series of crossed-out initials on its handle.

Goodie Whemper (maysherestinpeace). A research witch, so I gave her a certain air of dishevelled distraction from personal upkeep as her mind is on 'higher things'.

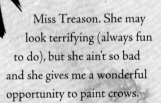

Miss Treason. She may look terrifying (always fun to do), but she ain't so bad and she gives me a wonderful opportunity to paint crows.

Mrs Earwig. I illustrate her with certain wizardly accoutrements such as stars on her hat. I indicate her condescending demeanour by giving her an exaggerated philtrum, as if there is a bad smell, and tight, disapproving lips (not to mention that eyeshadow).

Mrs Gogol, a voodoo witch. Terry drew on Creole and Cajun influences to depict this character, complete with her skilful cooking of jambalaya (which she then stares into to foretell the future). She lives in the Genua swamps, a Discworld parallel of the American Deep South. I illustrated this handsome woman with Creole earrings, a cowrie shell necklace and a headdress with crow's feathers and a ferret's skull.

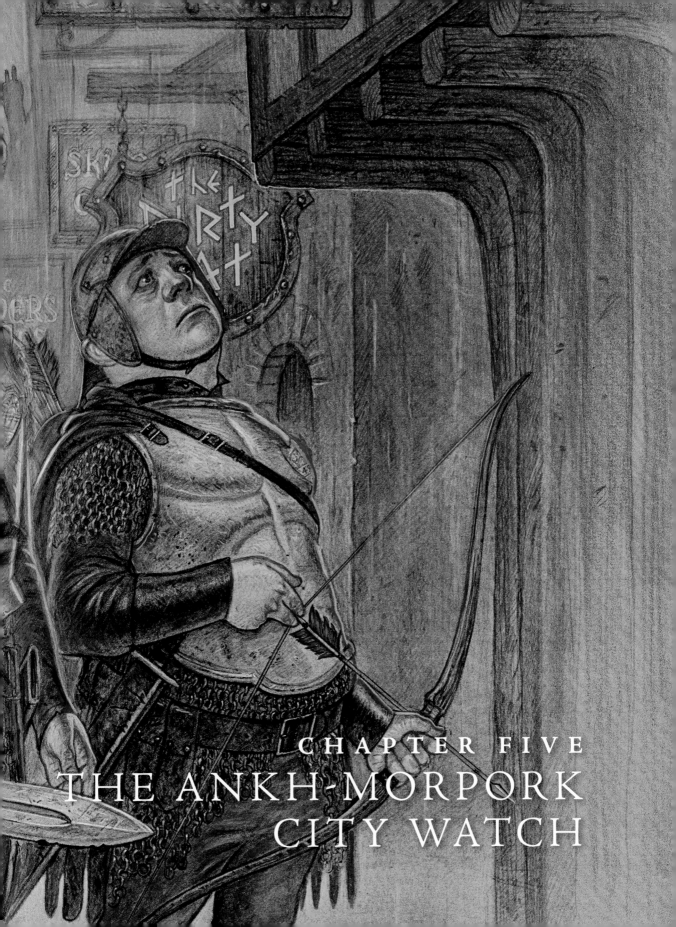

CHAPTER FIVE
THE ANKH-MORPORK
CITY WATCH

Looking back, I can see how much my renditions have developed over the years – as Terry's written depictions of these characters grew ever richer and more nuanced, I hope my own artwork kept up. The exaggerated features and almost cartoonish shapes have given way to more anatomically accurate renderings. Nobby remains a pleasing exception to this rule, defying human characteristics with aplomb. Yet however much has changed, many of the core aspects persist. The characters are still recognizable and retain unique details, such as their footwear – a narrative puzzle posed by Terry who first referred to them as 'sandals' and latterly as 'boots' which resulted in the Watch uniform boot/sandal hybrid which I think I may have been the first to visualize – however impractical this footwear might be in reality.

As the Watch grew, it became ever more important to differentiate each character visually – Terry creates very strong individuals and it's pleasing to echo their traits on the canvas: Nobby is shabby, his chainmail broken and unkempt, whilst Carrot's perfect armour shines (his codpiece has remained consistently present and eye-popping over thirty years of my drawing him), and Constable Visit's distinctive scaled armour and Sally's rerebraces hint at their different countries of origin.

THE CITY WATCH

The first time I drew the members of the Night Watch was for *The Pratchett Portfolio* in 1994. Led by the cynical Sam Vimes, this fantasy police force came about when Terry wanted to explore the hitherto nameless rank and file who would come running in a typical fantasy setting. *Guards! Guards!* introduced Vimes, Colon, Nobby and Carrot and each subsequent book has seen the ranks of the City Watch swell, with a new diversity of species and gender.

A note for pedants: Carrot is concussed, not drunk – perhaps a difficult distinction when illustrated.

Several versions of this illustration exist – it's continued to expand as the Watch itself has.

. . . a handful of unemployables who no one in their right mind could ever take seriously [. . .] And that was the Night Watch. Just the three* of them.

GUARDS! GUARDS!

Terry always maintained the Watch shouldn't have a uniform as such, but the challenge is trying to make them look like a cohesive group whilst still having a scavenged aesthetic to their armour. Besides medieval influences, the clothing in this piece also references First World War military uniforms, with leather straps.

* Four with the addition of Carrot

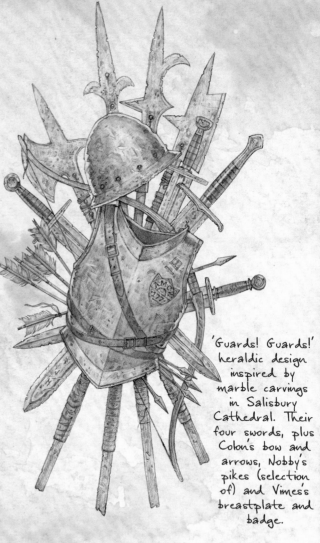

'Guards! Guards!' heraldic design inspired by marble carvings in Salisbury Cathedral. Their four swords, plus Colon's bow and arrows, Nobby's pikes (selection of) and Vimes's breastplate and badge.

An early rough for this composition

With all my full-colour pieces, I first sketch and work out the blocking and details in my trusty notebook. For any project, I typically have a long list of roughed-out ideas, many of which will never see the light of day; there are always too many ideas, too many gems from Terry's writing.

For this piece, *The Thin Brown Line*, I worked tonally in pencil, then built up atmospheric colour to emphasize the drizzly, murky street gleaming beneath magically glowing signs that advertise questionable and none-too-salubrious drinking establishments.

Terry described Vimes lighting his cigar with a hatchling swamp dragon, a gift for an illustrator!

SAM VIMES

Terry loved the Dirty Harry film series. The depiction of Captain Vimes in *Guards! Guards!* was therefore a perfect opportunity to draw a parallel to Harry Callahan, the alienated San Francisco cop of the movies. In typical Terry style he gave the film's infamous quotes a Discworld cod Latin mashup, thus evoking the classic Watch House motto: FABRICATI DIEM PVNC.

Vimes's character is very well defined right from the start as gritty, hard-drinking, cigar-smoking with little regard for police protocol. Despite there being little further physical description of Vimes than skinny and unshaven I felt that Clint Eastwood's Dirty Harry brought a strong visual starting point for the design of his appearance. Some years later, however, Terry gave me a note saying he imagined him as more of a Pete Postlethwaite type – so from then on, my illustrations channelled a bit of both actors to come up with a definitive version.

I enjoy realizing the world of the characters by designing objects and artefacts such as Vimes's Dragon's Blood Whiskey (every bottle matured for up to seven minutes).

'I've given that viewpoint a lot of thought, sir, and reached the following conclusion: arseholes to the lot of 'em, sir.'

FEET OF CLAY

91

Vimes remains one of my favourite characters; I never tire of following his story arc from a self-described drunk, haunting the grimy streets of Ankh-Morpork, to the contented and happily married man with the title His Grace Commander Sir Duke of Ankh and Head of the Ankh-Morpork City Watch. That said, the Vimes I most enjoy illustrating is his earlier, more rough-around-the-edges self, before the plumes and titles.

My first ever depiction of Vimes, drawn in 1994

This piece remains one of my favourites, as I feel it accurately portrays Vimes's discomfort with the rarefied situation he finds himself in.

Vimes's helmet has something of a classic British police helmet and of the Roundheads' helms from the English civil war – a deliberate nod to Vimes's own anti-monarchist ancestry.

Terry was never one to micromanage. He had strong opinions, which would often come down to telling me a character was 'right' or 'wrong', but he would never proverbially stand over my shoulder. The strength of the writing was always the best guide.

'This is Lord Mountjoy
Quickfang Winterforth IV,
the hottest dragon in the city.
It could burn your head
clean off.'

GUARDS! GUARDS!

The Summoning Dark, designed for
'Thud!', and one of the most popular
Discworld tattoos among fans. Terry
asked me to design this symbol - I
have pages and pages of ideas and
he opted for a circular design with
an eye and a tail.

This is one of the very few times I've deviated
from Terry's writing. Readers may remember
that the scene in 'Guards! Guards!' has
Vimes wearing one of Sybil's grandfather's
nightshirts.* Much as I love the visual, it's
a trifle difficult to explain when it's on the
front of a calendar.

*Plus Sybil's slippers with pink pompoms

93

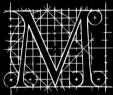y first Discworld novel cover was *Night Watch*. Up to then, almost all of Terry's Discworld novels in their UK editions had cover art by Josh Kirby. Josh had had an impressive artistic career illustrating science fiction and fantasy posters and books since the 1950s. I was long familiar with his flamboyant illustrative style, especially his 1979 film poster for *The Life of Brian*.

I first met Josh at a Discworld convention at the Adelphi Hotel, Liverpool, in 1998 where he was giving a talk and I was selling my early Discworld prints. He was a quiet man in double denim who was very friendly to me. We chatted about our surprise at the large turnout of fans and how neither of us was used to being in the public eye.

When Josh sadly passed away in 2001 Terry was writing his twenty-ninth Discworld manuscript with the working title *Forest of the Mind*. Terry invited me to his home and asked

if, in Josh's stead, I would like to create its cover. This was clearly a huge honour, not to mention responsibility; I had some very big boots to fill. As we discussed the story and possible cover concepts, I put forward the idea of creating a Discworld parody of Rembrandt's *The Night Watch*.

This mass portrayal by Rembrandt features real-life portraits of militiamen who had paid handsomely to be included in the work. My version features Discworld aficionados who bid in a charity auction to be included in the story. At the back, in the position where Rembrandt placed himself, I painted Josh Kirby as a tribute to him and his amazing contribution to the world of fantasy art. Terry decided to call the book *Night Watch*, which brought together the cover art and text harmoniously. Once submitted, the feedback from the publishers was that it was 'too brown', but it remains one of my favourites, and marked a turning point in my career. Initially some of the fans were confused by the change in cover artist,

'Don't put your trust in revolutions. They always come around
again. That's why they're called revolutions.
People die, and nothing changes.'

NIGHT WATCH

and some even thought that I had brutally usurped Josh rather
than the sad truth of his passing.

I think it is worth noting that Josh and I were at opposite
ends of our illustration careers when creating Discworld covers.
When Corgi, publishers of the paperbacks, commissioned
Josh to create a cover for *The Colour of Magic*, he was a long-
established fantasy artist with a huge back catalogue who was
being given a new unknown author. When I began working with
Terry the dynamic was reversed: I was the unknown and eager
artist open to discussion and author direction. Terry therefore
had a higher level of collaborative input with my artwork.

Despite the time constraints,
I made a detailed underpainting
before proceeding to full colour.

SYBIL RAMKIN

Early prototype drawings of Sybil were done in 1994. My first sketches of her have a large, rather masculine face with an exaggerated chin. These features were refined in 1995 for *The Pratchett Portfolio*. I initially took inspiration for this no-nonsense, upper-class woman from Geraldine James as Lady Maud Lynchwood in the TV series *Blott on the Landscape*; there is maybe a little Susan Sarandon in there as well.

Decades passed before I had opportunity to return to this hearty character. It was fun to rework her for the illustrated *Guards! Guards!*; I now depict her as less of a caricature with more subtle features. She still has a statuesque frame, a big chin, and a large wig but her impression is softer and more feminine. I hope she comes across as formidable but kind.

She had pages to herself in Twurp's Peerage, huge ancestral anchors biting into the past, and dwarfs also respected someone who knew their great-great-great-grandfather's full name.

THE FIFTH ELEPHANT

An early design for Lady Ramkin, complete with scorched leather apron and gauntlets

The curtain behind Sybil was inspired by the Arts and Crafts Movement, notably William de Morgan and William Morris. I created a heraldic dragon design for Sybil in a sumptuous blue for her grand abode, Ramkin House.

96

n illustration based upon the double portrait *Mr and Mrs Andrews* by society artist Thomas Gainsborough, painted in about 1750. Gainsborough's true passion was landscape painting, rather than being a portrait artist, which he disparagingly referred to as 'phizmonger'. This is evident in his beautiful rendition of the Andrewses' private estate. He famously wrote a letter in the 1760s claiming to be 'sick of portraits' and wanting to take his viola da gamba* into the countryside where he could paint landscapes. My version shows a contented Samuel and Sybil Vimes in a formal pose, overlooking the Ramkin estates with Ankh-Morpork on the horizon. In place of the dog, I included a swamp dragon.

The original shows a more complex relationship between the subjects, with Mrs Andrews giving the artist the side-eye while her husband looks less than thrilled beside her. Where Gainsborough included sheaves of corn to symbolize fertility, I've included craters to symbolize how explosive swamp dragons are. Gainsborough's sitters were only 16 and 22 at the time of painting, and the artist was 23. At that age, I was painting packaging for a company in Thornton Heath and driving an old brown Mini.

There are rumours that Gainsborough fell out with the couple mid-painting and that he hid some rude phallic symbolism in the work as revenge. I have done nothing of the sort in my version unless you count the Tower of Art in the background ...

*a stringed instrument like a small cello

Vimes murmured that he had occasionally seen society ladies with small, colourful dragons on their shoulders, and thought it looked very, er, nice.

'Oh, it sounds *nice*,' [Lady Ramkin] said. 'I'll grant you. Then they realize it means sootburns, frizzled hair and crap all down their back.'

GUARDS! GUARDS!

CAPTAIN CARROT

When depicting Carrot the main aim was to draw someone who looked honest – basically the other end of the spectrum from Nobby. He is described in the books as having red hair and a huge physique. I loosely based him originally on a young Liam Neeson but nowadays I think of him more like James Norton. I reasoned that as he is described as having a 'big honest face' he would therefore have an exaggerated chin akin to the classical depiction of a hero.

Carrot's badge number is 900; this references a song called 'The 900 Number' which is the B side of 'The King Is Here' by hip hop legend The 45 King. This is a rather convoluted deep dive and the sort of thing that amuses me.

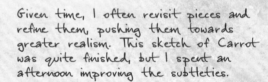

Given time, I often revisit pieces and refine them, pushing them towards greater realism. This sketch of Carrot was quite finished, but I spent an afternoon improving the subtleties.

'It's a nice sword,' [Colon] said thoughtfully. 'Well-balanced.'

'But not one for a king,' said Carrot. 'Kings' swords are big and shiny and magical and have jewels on and when you hold them up they catch the light, ting.'

GUARDS! GUARDS!

'Guards! Guards!' describes the somewhat nondescript, non-magical sword as 'a long piece of metal with very sharp edges. And it hasn't got destiny written all over it, so I inscribed the sword with runes that spell out 'hasn't got destiny'.

Besides his armour polish, Carrot has several other accessories: his belt contains a leather pouch with his notebook and pencil. The other notable feature is his 'protective', which Terry describes as 'a cross between a dessert bowl and a German helmet.'

STRONG IN THE ARM'S
ARMOUR POLISH
FOR GLEAMING SHORTS

SERGEANT COLON

My early designs of Colon drawn in 1994 show a rotund amiable chap. He is described as looking like a pork butcher, so I gave him a fleshy face with a high florid colour. Unlike the other guards in the Watch he wears Roman-style armour. He fits into the breast plate like a jelly in a jelly mould, complete with pectoral and abdominal muscles (not to mention nipples). His badge is number 49, which is in acknowledgement of *The Adventures of PC 49*, a 1949 British crime film based on a popular radio series that Terry enjoyed.

My latest versions of Colon show him with more than a passing similarity to John Henshaw.

It may be worth noting that I don't like or follow any sports . . . but I don't mind archery, which I have done occasionally. To me there is something rather zen about it. I therefore am happy to draw Colon's lucky arrow.

A million-to-one chance but it might just work . . .

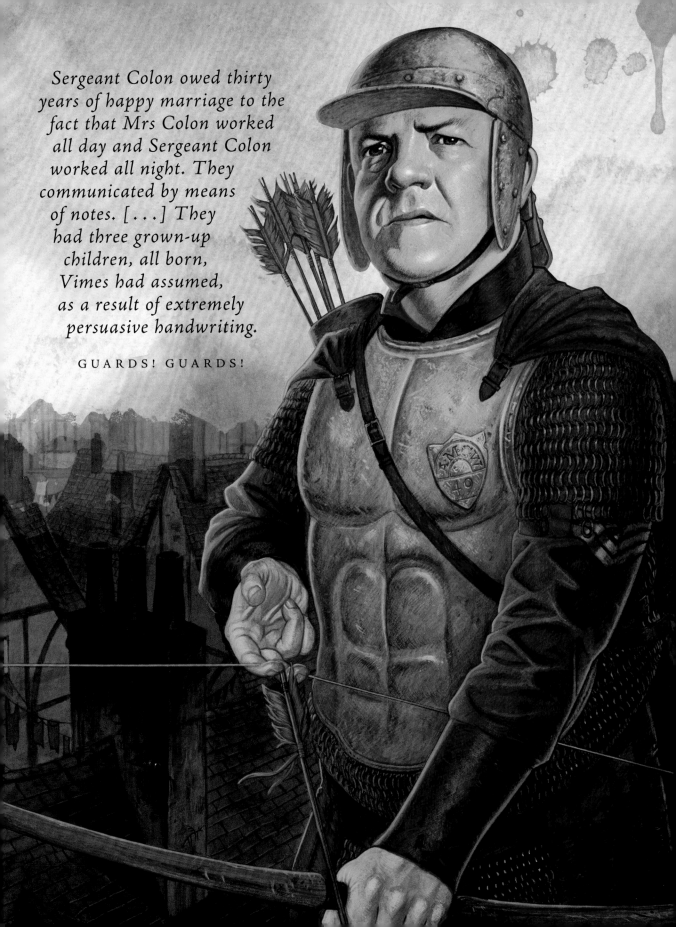

Sergeant Colon owed thirty years of happy marriage to the fact that Mrs Colon worked all day and Sergeant Colon worked all night. They communicated by means of notes. [...] They had three grown-up children, all born, Vimes had assumed, as a result of extremely persuasive handwriting.

GUARDS! GUARDS!

NOBBY NOBBS

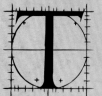

The original inspiration for Nobby's facial expressions was a young Phil Daniels as seen in the cult movie *Quadrophenia*. I drew him and brought in exaggerated elements of my own face. Terry was once asked 'Which character looks most like Paul?' and he replied 'Nobby', so he must have picked up on the aspect of self-portraiture. (Note he was not asked which character most smells like Paul.) I find it hard to stop drawing Nobby and have done him in various guises A LOT.

Nobby has become less hideous over the years that I've drawn him, maybe as a way to make him more likeable – despite his many, many flaws, there's something rather lovable about him.

Nobbs was a bit of a peacock. A very short peacock, it was true, a peacock that had been hit repeatedly with something heavy, perhaps, but a peacock nonetheless. It just went to show, you never could tell.

GUARDS! GUARDS!

Nearly naked Nobby

Nobby in chainmail

'Beti'

Nobby in PPE (a Covid painting)

Folk dancing Nobby

Nobby in Watch uniform

I, after hearing evidence from a number of experts, including Mrs. Slipdry the midwife, certify that the balance of probability is that the bearer of this document, C. W. St. John Nobbs, is a human being.

Lord Vetinari

I often illustrate Nobby with different badge numbers - I like to think he keeps a selection to hand, so as not to be easily identified . . .

Designing Nobby's mother was fun. She seems like a nice woman. I included pictures of Nobby and the Ankh-Morpork noble who is likely his father.

ANGUA

My early depictions of Angua resemble the comic-book style of female heroine. She is described as pretty but frankly back then I was more comfortable with drawing grotesque or humorous faces, rather than the fine features of an attractive woman, and so her features were more cartoony. Over the years I have worked on and developed this aspect of drawing and I now depict her as less of a caricature and with a more sensitive approach. My most recent painting of Angua, completed for a calendar and *The Ultimate Discworld Companion*, I view as definitive.

Being a werewolf meant having the dexterity and jaw power to instantly rip out a man's jugular. It was a trick of her father's that had always annoyed her mother, especially when he did it just before meals. But Angua had never been able to bring herself to do it. She'd preferred the vegetarian option.

MEN AT ARMS

I hope I've got better at designing women's faces, so I was really pleased to get to attempt this new image of Angua a few years ago.

DWARFS

On Discworld all dwarfs look male at first glance, regardless of their sex. For his universe, Terry was fascinated by deconstructing and then recreating fantasy staples, and his dwarfs are no exception. Dwarfs appear to be a monoculture, but in fact they diverge in interesting ways, across gender, tradition and occupation. It's a fun challenge to depict these differences.

A typical dwarf family, including a child dwarf, with chainmail mittens dangling out of his sleeves, looking very pleased with his rat on a stick.

The Knockerman. Depicting clothing that is taken to almost 'religious symbolism' appealed to me. I gave him multi-layered leather armour with lots of metal rivets for protection against unexpected explosions. The helmet has a narrow opening and a box for the firedamp-spotting cricket inside. The hammer is for knocking - obviously.

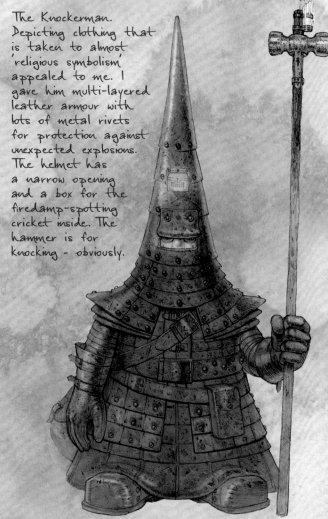

There aren't any Queens of the Dwarfs. Dwarfs are very reticent about revealing their sex, which most of them don't consider to be very important compared to things like metallurgy and hydraulics.

WITCHES ABROAD

Rat on a stick - a delicacy. Best with ketchup.

Grabpot Thundergust (left) embracing his dwarfish heritage with his oversized accessories. In contrast, Modo (below), the dwarf who looks after the gardens of Unseen University, is styled after a Victorian gardener.

When it came to Cheery Littlebottom, who openly identifies as female, it was fun to embrace the challenge of illustrating a female dwarf that looked feminine yet still presented typical dwarf attributes. It has been fascinating over the years to depict Cheery as an outwardly male dwarf gradually embracing and expressing her feminine side. I believe Terry was a champion of all types of people; his main talent was to gently poke fun at all of us and reflect our similarities rather than our differences.

Dwarf Bread - an opportunity to portray the most feared of the battle breads: dwarfish drop scones

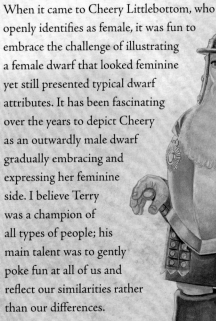

DETRITUS
AND OTHER TROLLS

Growing up I thought I might become a geologist as I was, and still am, fascinated by fossils, rocks and Earth science. I cannot resist collecting interesting flints, pebbles and stones when I am out walking and have a large collection at home which I use for reference.

A mimetolith is a natural rock feature that resembles a living form in nature, usually a face or creature, and, with a bit of imagination, it doesn't take much to turn my collection into illustrations of Discworld trolls. I enjoy this opportunity to bring to life different types of rock texture and formation. Trolls' faces are far more asymmetrical than humans', and I give them features such as broken noses, chipped teeth and scarring which indicates not only violent fighting but also millennia of weathering.

'Da Finker'

When Detritus first appears as a doorman for the Broken Drum tavern, he is recently arrived in Ankh-Morpork from the mountains of his origin. I depicted him as a hard, granite-type rock with outcrops of lichen and moss. As the books progress, he becomes a member of the City Watch and later illustrations show him moss-free from city living.

I've always been drawn towards illustrating humorous characters and situations but I have a particular philosophy about how best to do this. It's tempting to illustrate the 'punchline moment' where the joke comes to a head but, as Terry himself demonstrated countless times in his writing, it's much more satisfying for the reader to put the final piece together in their own heads. Therefore, a lot of my illustrations show the set-up rather than the denouement.

Trolls come in all shapes and sizes. Terry never describes the physical attributes of his characters at great length, but when he uses phrases like 'from the smoke, Ruby emerged like a galleon out of the fog', it's hard not to start visualizing. Terry created many trolls, both large and small. Like many aspects of his world, I sometimes find it hard to stop drawing.

A gnoll – a rubbish-collecting variety of troll. The eagle-eyed might spot the sonky amongst the items on his head.

The impressive Ruby

A yeti – a species of troll accustomed to the cold

Zorgo – a Retrophrenologist

The (comparatively) diminutive Asphalt, once sat upon by an elephant

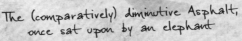

DISCWORLD PARODY: GIRL WITH A PEARL EARRING

'I like trolls,' said Twoflower.

'No you don't,' said Rincewind firmly. 'You can't. They're big and knobbly and they eat people.'

'No they don't,' said Cohen, sliding awkwardly off his horse and massaging his knees. 'Well-known mishapprehenshion, that ish. Trolls never ate anybody.'

'No?'

'No, they alwaysh spit the bitsh out. Can't digesht people, see?'

THE LIGHT FANTASTIC

nown as 'The Mona Lisa of the North', this work by Johannes Vermeer belongs to the Dutch Golden Age of painting and the style of portraiture is known as a tronie ('face' in the Dutch of that period).

Tronies depict anonymous sitters with idealized faces or exaggerated expressions and often feature outlandish accessories, like the turban and oversized earring (which would actually have been painted glass) worn by the girl. At the time of painting, the direct eye contact of the sitter was considered challenging and improper. Even the pearl earring itself had steamy overtones.

New scanning technology has revealed that the background used to be a green curtain, and that she had eyelashes that are now no longer visible because the paints have deteriorated over time.

Painting a parody with a Discworld spin has been something I've wanted to do for years, and picking a troll as the subject is about as far from the 'idealized form' as it's possible to get.

Terry writes about several trolls who, despite the modernizing and civilizing forces in troll society eschewing such things, still sport human bones as jewellery.

S W A M P   D R A G O N S

 wamp dragons are fun to draw. And draw. And draw . . . Swamp dragons are one of several Discworld creations that grew in the telling; Terry would react to my artwork and come back with new ideas based on what I had created. Most notably, the 'breeds of swamp dragon' page,

illustrated for *The Last Hero*, for which Terry provided suitably bizarre breed names and descriptions after seeing the finished piece.

The obvious starting point for swamp dragons was dogs – dragons on Discworld have complicated pedigrees and no shortage of accompanying ailments.

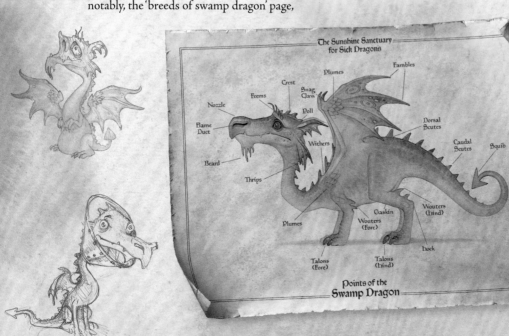

The Sunshine Sanctuary for Sick Dragons

Plumes
Fambles
Crest
Snag Claw
Feems
Poll
Nozzle
Flame Duct
Withers
Dorsal Scutes
Beard
Caudal Scutes
Squib
Thrips
Gaskin
Wouters (hind)
Plumes
Wouters (Fore)
Hock
Talons (Fore)
Talons (hind)

Points of the
Swamp Dragon

The temperature was terrible, but not as bad as the cocktail of smells. He staggered aimlessly from one metal-lined pen to another, while pear-shaped, squeaking little horrors with red eyes were introduced as 'Moonpenny Duchess Marchpaine, who's gravid at the moment' and 'Moonmist Talonthrust II, who was Best of Breed at Pseudopolis last year'.

GUARDS! GUARDS!

Hatchling swamp dragon designs, some of which later became sculptures.

DISCWORLD PARODY: LADY WITH AN ERMINE

The natural condition of the common swamp dragon is to be chronically ill, and the natural state of an unhealthy dragon is to be laminated across the walls, floor and ceiling of whatever room it is in. A swamp dragon is a badly run, dangerously unstable chemical factory one step from disaster. One quite small step.

MEN AT ARMS

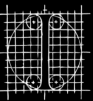

n Terry's twenty-fifth novel, *The Truth*, the Ankh-Morpork gangster Mr Tulip eyes up a painting titled *Woman Holding Ferret* by Leonard of Quirm. I imagine this was Terry drawing a Discworld parallel with *Lady with an Ermine* by Leonardo da Vinci. The original painting features the beautiful Cecilia Gallerani, the mistress of the Duke of Milan, Leonardo's patron at the time.

The venerable work is purported to have been 'restored' in Poland in the 1800s when Leonardo's blue-grey background was covered in darker paint and the erroneous title 'La Belle Ferronniere' and signature Leonard D'Awinci was added. To add insult to injury Leonardo's masterpiece was later

looted by the Nazis. Thankfully it was returned by the Monuments Men after the war.

My painting shows a well-dressed Ankh-Morpork lady holding a swamp dragon. Whilst not being the famed *Woman Holding Ferret* mentioned above, I imagine that this version was painted in Leonard of Quirm's 'Lady with …' period something akin to Picasso's blue period. My reason for not interpreting the work viewed by Mr Tulip is that a ferret is very like an ermine and therefore the parody would be verging on a copy of the original. My intention is to bring an additional element of humour and therefore I felt that a grand lady cuddling a swamp dragon would be more fitting, and who doesn't love a little dragon?

Errol in his original form (left), and his much later iteration

ERROL

Goodboy Bindle Featherstone of Quirm (also affectionately known as Errol) is technically a pedigree dragon. The first known dragon to flame from the 'other end'.

The poorly swamp dragon whose gradual recovery in *Guards! Guards!* echoes the transformation of Vimes and the City Watch as a whole, Errol is introduced in the story as a genetically disadvantaged young dragon prone to digestive problems. By the end he has transmogrified into a supersonic dragon who saves the day.

I first drew Errol in 1994 when I was working on *The Pratchett Portfolio*. I gave him teeth and scales similar to a crocodile, with huge nostrils, a pear-shaped body and eyebrows bigger than his wings.

In later renditions I gave him a longer snout following a discussion with Terry who suggested a similarity with the Concorde aircraft. I now paint him with drooping ears, larger eyes and less threatening teeth so his overall demeanour is more weirdly cute.

Never seen, but fun to imagine — Nobby's brother Errol, the dragon's namesake

Dear Paul,

Many thanks for your letter -- and Errol, of course, who is spot on (although I think his nose should extend further past the nostrils, like an organic Concorde...but I wouldn't argue much with your interpretation).

Terry's note about the original, sludge-coloured Errol (top left) and a subsequently redesigned Errol (top right)

Not such a big leap from whippet to whittle . . .

The biggest development in his overall design is that he is now less reptilian and more canine in body shape, thanks to my whippet who was an unwitting model. The collar and nametag also give him a more domesticated appearance. I first painted him a greenish-brown colour, akin to Pantone 448 C, dubbed 'the ugliest colour in the world'. I think my use of colour is one of the things that I have improved over the years and in later versions he is a more pleasant silvery green. In the most recent illustration he is zooming over Ankh-Morpork and has transformed, as described in the story, into a reflective chrome.

People ask me why I've illustrated Errol so many times. Who knows? Maybe it's because he rests at that happy crossroads, somewhere between dogs and dinosaurs.

Errol's pedigree certificate created for the Dunmanifestin edition of 'Guards! Guards!'

They were definitely dragons.
[. . .] But they resembled swamp
dragons in the same way that
greyhounds resembled those odd
yappy little dogs with lots of Zs
and Xs in their name.

THE LAST HERO

Moon dragons are described in 'The Last
Hero' as magnificent silver creatures,
propelled by a needle of blue flame
from their rear end. They gave me an
opportunity to design adult dragons that
are built for speed and look less pathetic
than their diminutive relatives on the Disc,
the swamp dragons.

'The Last Hero' also gave me the
opportunity to design space-faring dragons.
These are something like a whale with
small dragon-like wings for swimming
through the void.

120

NOBLE DRAGONS

Dragons crop up in most fantasy stories and are often on the shopping list of the genre as a quintessential ingredient. Discworld, of course, has dragons – and my approach is to try to bring something fresh with my illustrations whilst treading this familiar path. My noble dragons are rooted in dinosaur and crocodile anatomy, along with the long, horselike faces Terry described. Their large wings must be as believable as possible so that the concept of flight is not inconceivable, I studied the wings of bats and pterodactyls to understand the jointed anatomy and how it connects to the shoulder. The overall look of these creatures is very different to the swamp dragons of Discworld which have comedic physical absurdities; the noble dragon is far more majestic and serious, and potentially could eat you – or at least fry you alive.

A sooty silhouette where some residents of Ankh-Morpork met a fiery end. This is actually a parody of the album cover for 'Band on the Run' by Paul McCartney and Wings.

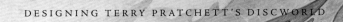

Noble dragons don't have friends. The nearest they can get to the idea is an enemy who is still alive.

GUARDS! GUARDS!

This is my first attempt at designing the noble dragon summoned by the Elucidated Brethren in 'Guards! Guards!'

123

've illustrated a good many Discworld covers and there's never been a specific formula for the content. Some feature memorable scenes from the book, others take a more metaphorical approach, visualizing the characters in imagined set-ups, but all were carefully planned and usually started with a suggestion from Terry.

For *Snuff*, I spoke to Terry, and he gave me a list of features he wanted to include. Terry told me he wanted Vimes steering a paddle boat through a gorge. Pursued by a tidal wave. And there should be lightning. And fallen branches . . . oh, and chickens.

Terry was always very generous in his estimation of my abilities, but this was certainly a healthy shopping list. Cover artwork has the added complication of requiring generous space for both the author's name and the book's title – a challenge that Josh Kirby also had to reconcile.

In the end, I jumped straight in with a pencil sketch, opting for a fish-eye lens approach, as a way of encompassing as much content as possible in the smallest space. The goblin was my addition (you can't go wrong with a goblin), though Terry asked that I make him less 'pointy' in the final version, to convey a more benign presence.

My approach for a piece this frenetic is to carefully limit the colour palette, to make it easier for the eye to decrypt – though Terry's initial response upon seeing the cover was to drily remark that I must have a big pot of 'Kidby blue' paint I'd been looking to use up.

When I submitted the finished artwork, the publishers requested one final addition – waves crashing over the deck.

THE
ELUCIDATED
BRETHREN
OF THE EBON NIGHT

This group of disgruntled tradesmen dressed in pseudo ceremonial robes was inspired by a photograph I came across of a local group who may or may not have a special line in handshakes. I persuaded my wife and our colleague to dress in *Star Wars* Jedi robes and have their photos taken in the garden to provide me with visual reference for the folds of the fabric. In the eventual painting four of the Brethren are based on art director Alex, the reluctant model with folded arms is my wife, and I posed for the figure in the centre. It's all in a day's work . . .

Their banners were fun to design and feature the Universal Lemon along with a selection of the mystical symbols for fire and brimstone as well as salt and vinegar.

They are standing on a chalked design which is used for summoning the dragon that terrorizes Ankh-Morpork. I spent hours creating a dragon-rune cypher that surrounds the octogram. This translates as 'Here be Dragons'.

Much fun was had creating propaganda for the Brethren – complete with claims to make 'Ankh-Morpork great again' . . .

'Is the Door of Knowledge sealed fast against heretics and knowlessmen?'

'Stuck solid,' said Brother Doorkeeper. 'It's the damp. I'll bring my plane in next week.'

GUARDS! GUARDS!

A door inspired by St Anthony's Church on the Roseland in Cornwall

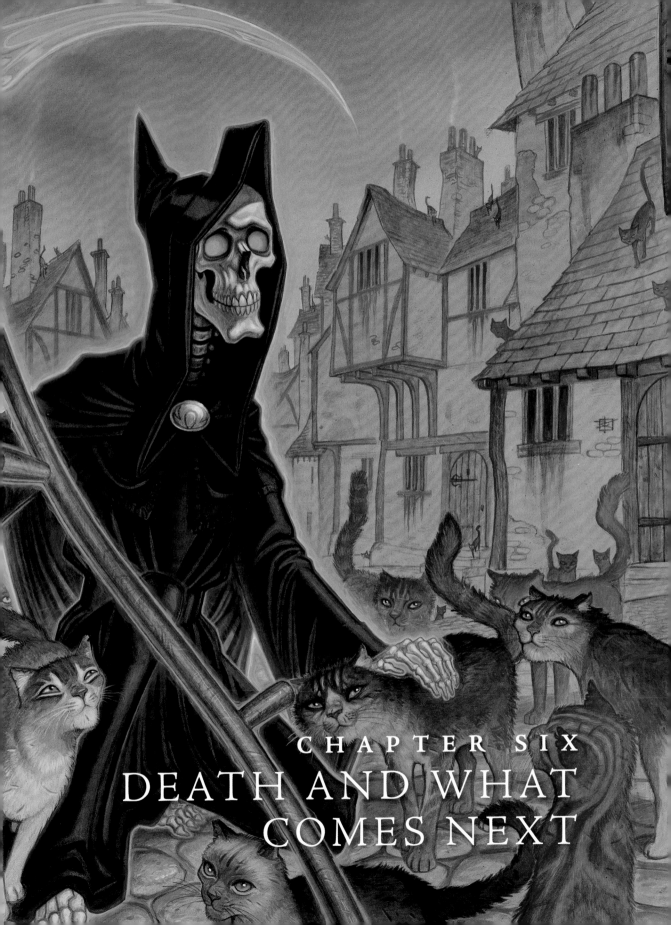

CHAPTER SIX
DEATH AND WHAT
COMES NEXT

The fishing fly 'Death's Glory'. While aspiring to make all of my pieces aesthetically pleasing, I tried to make the fly look 'primordial' and - as Terry observed - as if it 'had bred on mammoth turds'.

DEATH

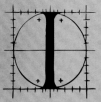

I am not alone in being particularly fond of the Discworld Death character: the readership has taken him to their hearts. The challenge when drawing him is to show a kindly nature on a bony skull. I am working against the traditional and ancient preconception of Death, trying to flip the iconic image of the forbidding and scary Grim Reaper.

I began designing this character with observational studies using an artist's anatomical model of a skull. I created three tonal sketches on grey paper observing the form from various angles.

Once I was familiar with the characteristics of the skull, I was then able to develop the look for Death by exaggerating and stretching elements of it. My design features an elongated lower half, from brow to chin, in keeping with his great seven-foot height.

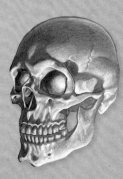

A typical skull has the 'grin' but not the benign look of Death.

Death's blade – a bastard sword with a diamond cross section, an Omega on the cross guard and a bone handle.

Death's brows are tilted up in a quizzical manner as he is bemused by the activities of humankind. I give a soft blue glow to the eye sockets; this initially graduated from a light centre to dark edge, but I now paint it as if the blue glow is illuminating the socket with blue right to the edge.

I always give him good strong teeth, perhaps as a nod to my days making dentures.

His cowl is always pointed which also exaggerates his height.

Terry described Death as having a silver cloak fastening embossed with the Omega symbol to represent 'the end'. I designed this in an art nouveau style inspired by Alphonse Mucha. On one occasion I also gave him an Omega ring but decided not to include it in further renditions.

Any excuse to draw Death is also potentially an excuse to draw a cat.

'What is there in this world that makes living worth while?'

Death thought about it.

CATS, he said eventually, CATS ARE NICE.

SOURCERY

132

Death with Mort, his
apprentice

> *The lifetimers of most people were the classic shape that Death thought was right and proper for the task. They appeared to be large eggtimers, although, since the sands they measured were the living seconds of someone's life, all the eggs were in one basket.*
>
> THE LAST CONTINENT

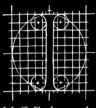 have always been inspired by the master of graphic impossibility M. C. Escher, and this is not the first time I have taken inspiration from his work. In 2021 I illustrated 'The Librarian Lost in L-Space' which paid conceptual homage, most notably, to the *House of Stairs*, which he drew in 1951 and is typical of his picture puzzles.

Skeletal Hand with Lifetimer is a more direct parody of his 1935 lithograph *Hand with Reflecting Sphere (Self-Portrait in Spherical Mirror)*. The original shows a human hand holding a sphere in which we can see the artist himself captured with a fish-eye perspective.

My interpretation shows the skeletal hand of Death and the sphere reflects Death seated in his study accompanied by the Death of Rats.

It is not only Escher's skill as a draughtsman I admire, I also applaud his work ethic as revealed in a letter to his son Arthur in 1955.

'Talent and all that for the most part is nothing but hogwash. Any schoolboy with a little aptitude might very well draw better than I perhaps; but what he most often lacks is the tough yearning for realization, the teeth-grinding obstinacy and saying: even though I know I'm not capable of it, I'm still going to do it.'

n 2011 a French publisher commissioned a painting of Terry with his Discworld character Death. It offered a perfect opportunity to execute an idea that had been forming in my mind for a while. Knowing that one of Terry's favourite films was *The Seventh Seal*, it seemed apt to parody the scene where the knight, Antonius Block, plays chess with Death. Terry was battling Alzheimer's by the time I created this work, which gave the painting an emotive dimension, although this wasn't part of my original idea. I worked out the chess moves (with pieces inspired by the Isle of Lewis set), so that Terry is positioned on the board to win.

Ingmar Bergman was himself inspired by a medieval mural in the vault of the parish church of Täby, near Stockholm, created in 1480 by the German-born artist Albrekht Ymmenhusen, known as Albertus Pictor, renowned for his mural paintings in Sweden. It depicts a man losing a game of chess against a figure personifying Death.

REMIND ME AGAIN,
[*Death*] *said*, HOW THE
LITTLE HORSE-SHAPED
ONES MOVE.

SMALL GODS

'Take off that mask!'

AS YOU WISH. I DO LIKE
TO GET INTO THE SPIRIT
OF THE THING.

*The figure removed
its mask.*

'And now take off that other
mask!' said Salzella, as the
frozen fingers of dread rose
through him.

MASKERADE

*He's Checking
His List: My
illustration for
the Hogfather's
outfit is inspired
by Thomas Nast's
designs from the
late 1800s.*

 erry's writing pushes Death
into new situations and
similarly pushed me in my
depictions of the reaper.
Death regularly takes on
new, temporary, personas – often because the
plot demands that such a powerful character be
removed from his comfort zone.

Bill Door is a somewhat perplexed Death in
dungarees who is experiencing the confusing joys
of being human. I have given him an outfit akin
to a 1930s American farmer: overalls, a cotton
neckerchief and straw hat. I used to watch *The
Waltons* on TV when I was growing up and liked
their country aesthetic.

My interpretation of
Death from Masquerade
draws its influence from
Lon Chaney's costume
in the 1925 black and
white film version of
Phantom of the Opera.
I painted him flame
red, as described by
Terry, which also draws
a parallel with
'The Masque of
the Red Death' by
Edgar Allan Poe

DEATH'S DOMAIN

Death lives on an astral plane all his own. He carefully apes many of the elements of human dwellings – with a distinct taste for the twee – but without properly understanding their context. Whenever possible, I embellish Death's possessions with recurring Omega motifs and bone shapes.

Illustrating the world of Death allows me a freedom to step in a more surreal direction, and the limited colour palette makes for an interesting challenge, which I interpret through the addition of subtle blues and purples.

When it came to creating Death's house, 'Mon Repos', I looked at the vernacular style of an Edward Lutyens cottage. I gave it tall chimneys, a steeply multi-angled pitched roof, beams and lead-paned windows. This all brings to mind the quintessential English country home (but in black).

Like all beekeepers, Death wears a veil.

When it came to designing Death's garden gnomes, the challenge was to make the traditional rounded figure of the garden gnome appear skeletal. It is in fact a classic Terry trait!

We are all familiar with the friendly-looking ornaments in our nans' gardens – bearded, tubby and rosy-cheeked, often pushing a wheelbarrow or holding a spade. They were historically used in gardens to protect the plants, keep evil spirits away and ensure a bountiful harvest. I decided not to give Death's gnomes beards as it looked too incongruous, and instead of rosy cheeks I exaggerated their cheekbones to make them more rounded and 'jolly'. They wear classic hooded cowls which have been stretched and overstated as a reflection of the gnomes' traditional pointy caps.

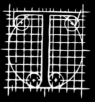he eminent Victorian and key figure of the Arts and Crafts Movement William Morris created the repeating textile design of the 'Strawberry Thief' in 1883 after watching the thrushes stealing berries from his kitchen garden at his country home, Kelmscott. The birds in the design were drawn by his close friend, architect Philip Webb. It marked a triumph in Morris's hand block-printing process as he perfected his complex indigo-discharge print method with which he had been heartily absorbed. His friend Walter Crane recalled 'hearing a strong cheery voice call out: "I'm dyeing, I'm dyeing, I'm dyeing!"'

When Morris was experimenting with his dye technique, according to Henderson's biography his 'hands and arms up to the elbow [were] permanently blue'. 'Strawberry Thief' has been commercially successful ever since, and is used on wallpapers, fabric and homewares.

Death in Discworld is known to have a comfortable and 'stylish' home complete with a grandfather clock, sweeping staircases and garden gnomes outside. Inspired by my wife's late grandmother who had a bedroom excessively wallpapered and curtained in a pink version of the 'Strawberry Thief', I created the chez Death version. This depicts a skeletal thrush eating black strawberries amongst the creeping foliage intertwined with a skull motif, apposite for the master bedroom of the Grim Reaper.

It's surely only a matter of time before someone wants to do Discworld wallpaper – quite a long time, I hope.

TERRY PRATCHETT

(sorry Terry!)

THE
DEATH OF RATS

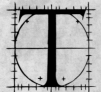his began as a minor character that became rather more. Terry was amused by the Death of Rats and his cheerful nature and own dialogue. My job was to make him an endearing 'mini me' to accompany the human-shaped Death. I began by observing and sketching the skulls of rats, but these did not quite capture the cheeky aspects of the character I was after. So, instead I used a rabbit's skull as my starting point for the design. This has larger eye sockets and more defined teeth, so the shape is more clearly interpreted.

Matching his counterpart, the Death of Rats has an Omega brooch and scythe. Luckily, I had a friend who supplied me with rodent skulls and an antique scythe handle which helped my research. I put a lot of value in what is termed as 'primary resource material' – also known as drawing from life, even when designing Death.

The Death of Rats holding sheep's eyeballs.* Originally drawn in pencil for the Special Nibbles** section of *Nanny Ogg's Cookbook*. This illustration is oddly popular, so I painted a colour version for *The Discworld Imaginarium*.

*Sheep's eyes are unusual because they have a rectangular shaped pupil, as do those of the octopus and horse.

**A side note for those concerned is that the 'eyeball' in the recipe comprises a pickled onion, cream cheese and an olive.

Observational studies of a rat skull and rabbit skull. The rabbit, I think you will agree, has a more winning smile.

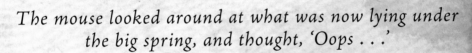

The mouse looked around at what was now lying under the big spring, and thought, 'Oops . . .'

Then its gaze went up to the black-clad figure that had faded into view by the wainscoting.

'Squeak?' it asked.

SQUEAK, said the Death of Rats.

And that was it, more or less.

HOGFATHER

For pose and anatomical reference, I used a copy of a nineteenth-century plaster horse by Domenico Brucciani.

B I N K Y

 y painting of Death on Binky was created in 2000 on a very large (4ft x 3ft) piece of MDF. However, once framed and behind glass it makes it a rather heavy work to hang. In the early days I had sometimes painted on bits of hardboard from my dad's shed and MDF presented a similar familiar surface whilst being more robust and larger than any illustration board available. In hindsight stretched, primed canvas would have been better but at this point I had not had the opportunity to work on canvas and did not have the time to experiment with it. Nowadays my larger works are more often on primed canvas and it is a lovely surface to paint on.

My more recent artworks show a better working knowledge of horses' anatomy and tack.

Now I live near the New Forest I have much better access to directly observe horses and ponies and am able to make drawings from life.

The horse's name was Binky. He was a real horse. Death had tried fiery steeds and skeletal horses in the past, and found them impractical, especially the fiery ones, which tended to set light to their own bedding and stand in the middle of it looking embarrassed.

REAPER MAN

I looked at photographs by Patrick Gries in 'Evolution in Action' and drawings in 'The Anatomy of the Horse' by the equine master artist George Stubbs (1724-1806). Without good reference undertaking drawings such as this would not be possible.

Binky is described as a living, breathing white stallion with uncanny powers of speed and longevity. I have chosen the Lipizzaner breed when depicting him: this is a long-lived powerful baroque type known for its beauty and white coat.

Death has two kittens in his saddlebag, and the Death of Rats rides between Binky's ears, subtle indicators of his benevolent nature.

THE FOUR HORSEMEN

Albrecht Dürer, one of my artistic heroes, illustrated the four horsemen as a woodcut in 1498 as part of his apocalypse series. This was my starting point to design these characters for Discworld. When Dürer created his work, people were fearful that the world might come to an end in the year 1500. There was a similar feeling of foreboding about the turn of the millennium when I created this piece.

I painted this sizeable work in oils in the summer of 1999. It was used as the promotional image for *The Last Hero*, which was released in 2001. The four horsemen seemed an apt choice of subject for that particular moment. Despite being primarily created for *The Last Hero* the illustration was used (unfinished) in the Discworld calendar for that year, and then because it had already been published, to my disappointment, Terry decided not to include it in *The Last Hero*.

LET ME SEE, NOW. THAT'S A — WHAT WAS IT AGAIN?

'A Bloody Mary.' This voice made a simple drinks order sound like the opening of hostilities.

OH, YES. AND—

'Mine was a small egg nog,' said Pestilence.

AN EGG NOG.

'With a cherry in it.'

SOURCERY

OTHER HORSEMEN

Terry, not content with just four horsepeople of the apocalypse, added Kaos, the fifth horseman: by day Ronnie Soak the milkman. Ronnie's alter ego wears a Trojan-inspired outfit with the Mandelbrot set engraved on his helmet, sword and shield to represent the pattern of chaos.

Reaper Man introduced New Death, a variant of the Grim Reaper. He is described as faceless; this is an illustrative challenge when the defining characteristics cannot be portrayed through the plasticity of facial features. I began by photographing rising smoke and looking at the organic forms of spiky twisted wood for the crown on his brow. His scythe is based on sharp, bleached wood which has a resemblance to splintered bones. I gave him exaggerated long fingers with bony joints bandaged in black cloth akin to a mummy.

An early design for Ronnie Soak. He ended up looking more human, though I do have a soft spot for this slightly goblinesque version.

Meat Loaf
BAT OUT OF HELL

SONGS BY JIM STEINMAN

Carefully airbrushing the blue glow, after having sprayed the poisonous cadmium red outside . . .

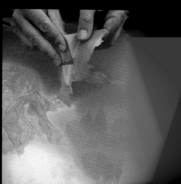

Painstakingly peeling off the mask . . .

Painting all the fine detail by hand.

merican illustrator and comic-book artist Richard Corben created the album cover artwork for Meat Loaf's debut album, *Bat Out of Hell*, in 1977. The image features a motorbike, ridden by a long-haired man, bursting out of the ground in a graveyard. Terry describes a scene in *Soul Music* when Death surfaces from the cellars of Unseen University, wrecking Modo's prized rose garden, clearly evoking this album cover. I painted this parody for the 2011 Discworld calendar and enjoyed replicating the various techniques used including airbrushing and blowing thinned paint with a straw to create the trees. It was Terry's request for 'Bat Out of Hell' to be played at his funeral.

Modo had a brief vision of flames and something arcing into the sky before his vision was blotted out by a rain of beads, feathers and soft black petals.

He shook his head, and ambled off to fetch his shovel.

QUOTH

I was a bit of a twitcher as a boy and would cycle up to Rickmansworth on my mum's shopper to watch birds. So, I especially enjoy drawing and painting members of the avian world and will take the opportunity if I can.

Quoth serves as the mount for the Death of Rats. Despite his intelligence he appears as a typical raven with a knowing beady eye. My early illustrations of him give him ragged and scruffy feathers; he looks tidier in a later version painted for *The Ultimate Discworld Companion*, Dunmanifestin edition.

The challenge is to create the feathered form in tones of black with added highlights. I use a combination of Mars Black paint with a mix of Ultramarine Violet and Raw Umber.

For a vegetarian, I find myself illustrating a lot of eyeballs . . .

The wizard who thought he owned him called him Quoth, but that was only because he didn't have a sense of humour and, like most people without a sense of humour, prided himself on the sense of humour he hadn't, in fact, got.

SOUL MUSIC

Quoth isn't the only bird on the Disc. There are few projects where I don't find an excuse to illustrate a feathered character or two – Terry, who had a great appreciation for the natural world, included a surprising number of birds across Discworld. I've always had a fondness for birds. I have a childhood memory of feeding the pigeons in Trafalgar Square and the sparrows in St James's Park; both were happy avian experiences that consolidated my love of all birds. It was for me the 1970s London equivalent of swimming with dolphins!

ALBERT

My initial inspiration for this character was Wilfrid Brambell from *Steptoe and Son*, as requested by Terry.

As Death's servant he is known for his culinary skills with a frying pan (fried porridge anyone?), his roll-up cigarettes and lack of general hygiene and good manners. I depict him with a perpetual drip on his nose, red-rimmed eyes and an unshaven chin. His posture is stooped, and he wears the waistcoat and breeches of a Victorian farm worker, complete with carpet slippers and fingerless gloves.

I have yet to draw him smiling but if I ever do his teeth will be as stained, crooked and mossy as old tombstones.

A concept for the statue of Alberto Malich, as he once was: founding Archchancellor of Unseen University

Albert was bent over the stove. 'Morning,' he said, [. . .] 'You want fried bread with your sausages? There's porridge to follow.'

Susan looked at the mess sizzling in the huge frying pan. It wasn't a sight to be seen on an empty stomach, although it could probably cause one.

SOUL MUSIC

154

MORT

❧

Terry had requested that Death's former apprentice be dressed in pantaloons. This led me to depict him in Elizabethan-style black doublet and hose, complete with a codpiece. He wears a hooded cape akin to his master's cowl and carries the tools of his trade, namely sword, scythe and hourglass. His physique is youthful and gangly in my early drawings.

My sketch of young Mort, who looks not dissimilar to me in my youth, although I never sported the 1970s perm.

SUSAN

D eath's granddaughter was described by Terry as a 'kind of Goth Mary Poppins' and he approved of the 'steel magnolia' look which I bestow on her. Her distinguishing feature is her hair which is described like a dandelion seed head, white with a streak of black. Her stance is upright and confident as befits a relative of Death.

Her costume, like her parents', is based in the Elizabethan era, but I then gave it a twist to reflect her youth and single-minded attitude. Her skirt is therefore tighter-fitting with a split at the side and her lace-up boots are long and yet sensible to match her practical nature. I have also drawn her in a high-necked blouse, long skirt and a Victorian-style riding coat which seems to suit her level-headed outlook and to be the right garb (complete with a poker) for seeing off Bogeymen. As with her grandfather, I always give her, and the other members of Death's Domain who help carry out scythe duties, an otherworldly glow in Phthalo Blue paint.

MISS FLITWORTH

The no-nonsense and stoic spinster of *Reaper Man* who as a young woman overcame the loss of her fiancé on the eve of their wedding day. She spent her life farming on the Octarine Grass Country and in her twilight years she employed Bill Door (Death), who was sufficiently impressed by her to allow her soul to remain in the world just long enough to attend the village dance.

I first designed Miss Renata Flitworth for the drawing *Discworld Gothic* in 2004, which parodies the famous American work of art by Grant Wood. I painted a colour version of this ten years later and the original now hangs in Terry's office.

I strive to keep her visual appearance different from Granny Weatherwax's, as they share a similar stature, dress sense and firm expression. Miss Flitworth's tanned and wrinkled 'like a walnut' face shows she is accustomed to the outdoor life, dealing with animals and farm work, which belies the underlying grit of her nature. Strong brows and unfussy white hair also reflect this. Her expression is that of one who has known sorrow and got on with life regardless. Her cameo-style brooch has a rose design because Death names one of the roses in his garden after her.

You know when you said that seeing me gave you quite a start?

'Yes?'

It gave you quite a stop.

REAPER MAN

LORD, WHAT CAN THE HARVEST HOPE FOR,
IF NOT FOR THE CARE OF THE REAPER MAN?

REAPER MAN

My painting of Death (as Bill Door) with Miss Flitworth joins the ranks (from *The Rocky Horror Picture Show* to *SpongeBob SquarePants*) that pay homage to Grant Wood's *American Gothic*, painted in 1930. Death appears more jovial than the dour farmer in the original – I gave him an ear of corn held between his teeth and his scythe is carried jauntily over his shoulder. The Death of Rats can be seen on the porch of the house, which is in the 'Carpenter Gothic' architectural style – thus giving both paintings their titles.

CHAPTER SEVEN

TIFFANY ACHING AND THE FEEGLES

Paul's image of her is definitive – you can see defiance just edging ahead over fear.

TERRY PRATCHETT

The Tiffany books give me the opportunity to paint elements of the chalk downs which I enjoy. These include swallows, Chalk Hill Blue butterflies and the chalk horse which is closely aligned to that of the prehistoric Uffington hill figure on the Oxfordshire downs.

TIFFANY ACHING

❧ ⬧ ❧

The main challenge when drawing versions of Tiffany is to show her growing up. My first drawings are of her aged nine in *The Wee Free Men* with big boots and a defensive frying pan. My later illustrations show her as a young woman embarking on her calling as a country witch on the Chalk. I always try to give her a look of determination with a steady gaze and an upright posture to reflect her courage despite often facing scary situations.

Over the years I have developed a softer approach to depicting the delicate features of her face. This is by using very subtle shading to capture the contours of her youthful appearance. In order to age her I gradually elongated the shape of her face and the length of her nose, making her features slightly more angular as she matures.

Of all my designing for Discworld I have probably done the most for the five books in the Tiffany Aching series which I also feel was, alongside *The Last Hero*, my most collaborative phase working with Terry.

Over the years I have designed covers for the hardbacks, paperbacks and (my favourite) gift editions of this set of stories. They gave me an opportunity to draw the flora and fauna of the chalk alongside its witches.

I did colour roughs for all of the Tiffany paperbacks, to try to make sure I got the tone exactly right in the finished piece.

An early rough for 'The Wee Free Men'. Miss Tick was later removed - my original plan for the covers was to pair Tiffany with a different elder witch on each.

The final pencil for the gift edition of 'A Hat Full of Sky'

It's been quite a few years since I painted the original cover for 'A Hat Full of Sky', but it does evoke one very clear memory: upon showing Terry the finished piece, he exclaimed that it was the first time I'd ever brought him a cover BEFORE the deadline and he insisted on taking a photo to commemorate the unusual occurrence.
Always the comedian.

164

I enjoyed selecting key elements
from the stories to draw as chapter
headings. Terry himself initially sketched
the land under the wave design (above)
with a biro on a scrap of paper.

Having lived just along the valley from Terry in the Cranborne Chase Area of Outstanding Natural Beauty, I know well the green landscape that was the inspiration for the Discworld Chalk country. It consists of rolling, rabbit-nibbled grasslands with far-reaching views, ancient woodlands and clear chalk streams. It is also an international dark sky reserve as there is no light pollution. Both Terry and I were drawn to the geology of the area as, having been the seabed millions of years ago, it is fossil-rich and flinty. Neolithic earthworks dot the hilltops. These prehistoric remains provided the inspiration for the home of the Nac Mac Feegle clan, who live below the turf in the ancient burial mound of a king.

Both Roundworld and Discworld chalklands have chalk figures known as geoglyphs carved into the hillsides. The art of carving white horses into chalk upland areas is known as leucippotomy and a relative of the Bronze Age Uffington White Horse is transported into Terry's writing.

The concept of the Long Man in Lancre shares DNA with the Cerne Abbas Giant that presides over a Dorset village.

Down in the valleys are farmsteads and villages where life has changed very little over the centuries, much like in Tiffany's world where the economy runs on sheep – namely wool, cheese and mutton. Illustrating the Chalk is always a favourite theme for me to return to – not least the buzzards, butterflies and hares that live there. Not to mention the Nac Mac Feegles, of course, who I never tire of.

They flowed out of Granny Weatherwax's hive, circling Tiffany like a halo, crowning her, and swarm and girl stood on the threshold of the cottage and Tiffany reached out her arms and the bees settled along them, and welcomed her home.

THE SHEPHERD'S CROWN

When I received the call telling me that Terry had passed away, I was working on this drawing. I think this explains Tiffany's expression: my sadness was reflected in the work.

In this version I gave her a crown of bees rather than her usual witch's hat, which is a tribute to Granny Weatherwax. This drawing marks the end of my collaboration with Terry and, personally, I feel this image is more poignant than the final revised cover which was done as requested by the publishers.

In the revised jacket design for *The Shepherd's Crown*, Terry's final book, which was published posthumously, Tiffany is depicted as a young woman wearing her traditional witch's hat and looking happier than my original drawing. She has a single bee on the palm of her hand.

The publishers asked me to remove additional bees that were painted on her hands and arms. Traces of these can still be faintly seen on her skin. This is an example of pentimento, which is the term used for changes made during the process of painting that are hidden beneath subsequent paint layers.

The very first design I committed to my sketchbook for 'The Shepherd's Crown'

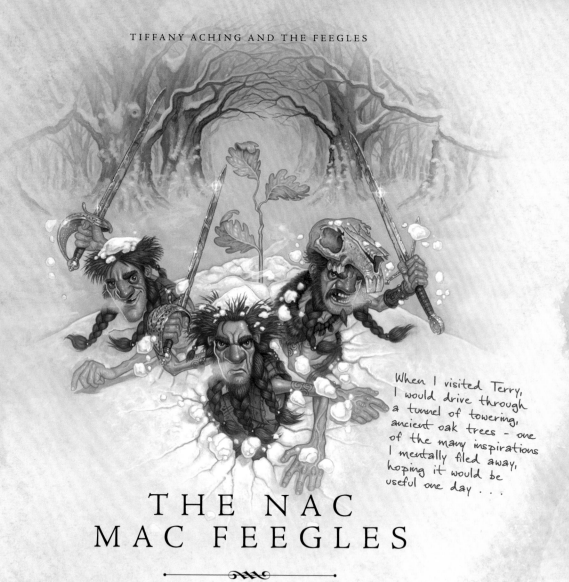

When I visited Terry, I would drive through a tunnel of towering, ancient oak trees – one of the many inspirations I mentally filed away, hoping it would be useful one day . . .

THE NAC MAC FEEGLES

osh Kirby illustrated the Nac Mac Feegle Long Lake Clan for the cover of *Carpe Jugulum* in 1998. These were portrayed, as described, as little men in pointed blue caps, akin to body-building Smurfs. I also painted these captivating characters in the same year after reading the novel and felt compelled to visually reimagine them. In my resulting mass portrait of battle-ready tribal pictsies all have red hair, tattooed blue skin, broken noses and missing teeth. They are scrawny, with big knuckles, knees

and elbows – useful for fighting. They belligerently stare directly out at the viewer with an attitude that is fierce and rebellious and, taking inspiration from *Braveheart* and *Trainspotting*, definitely Scottish. Unusually, for me, I disregarded the description in the text that they wore little blue hats and instead gave some of them animal skull helmets of rabbit, crow and weasel.

I took my finished painting to show Terry who, thankfully, liked my somewhat off-piste depiction of his characters. He bought the work and hung it up in his office.

Terry coined the word 'spickle' – to describe nasal and ear hair – I was rather taken with this and created a Feegle with plenty of both.

Note the Feegles' swords glow blue when close to Toad – a lawyer in his previous incarnation.

The Chalk Hill Blue butterfly is a real butterfly, native to the chalk downs, which I include frequently in artwork depicting the Chalk.

Three years later, when Terry was writing *The Wee Free Men*, and had commissioned me to create the cover art, he pointed to my *Feegle Horde* painting and singled out the fellow with the plaited beard. 'That is Rob Anybody, leader of the clan,' he told me. I therefore painted the same character front and foremost for *The Wee Free Men* jacket. I also included myself, brandishing a paintbrush rather than a sword at the back of the group. I enjoyed including natural details indigenous to the landscape such as the tiny flint arrow heads and a Chalk Hill Blue butterfly.

Over the years I have drawn countless variations of these diminutive warriors and, although some of them have had haircuts, they have changed little from that first illustration which inspired Terry.

Illustrating the Feegles' matriarch, the Kelda, was one of those times when it all went well! She made me smile as she appeared on my page.

An early sketch for Rob Anybody. He sports a black eye and a cheery grin.

172

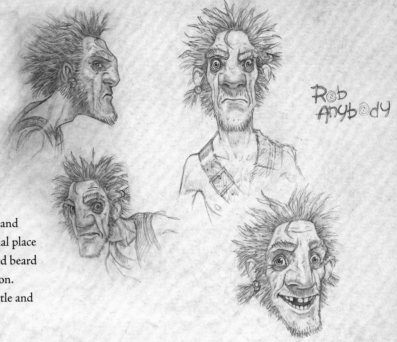

Rob Anybody, the drinking, stealing and scrapping leader of the clan, has a special place in my heart. I initially gave him a plaited beard and sidelocks and a very fierce expression. Nowadays Rob's look has softened a little and has an appearance of exuberant joy.

'Whut's the plan, Rob?' said one of them.

*'OK, lads, this is what we'll do.
As soon as we see somethin',
we'll attack it. Right?'*

THE WEE FREE MEN

The drawing that began my development of the look of the Nac Mac Feegles was one made in 1998 (left), after reading *Carpe Jugulum*, a rough sketch of what became Rob Anybody. This acted as something of a catalyst and quickly led to my colour painting *The Feegle Horde* (p. 171). The 'gnome' Wee Mad Arthur (below), a rat catcher in *Feet of Clay*, who later transpires to be Feegle-born, also developed over the years.

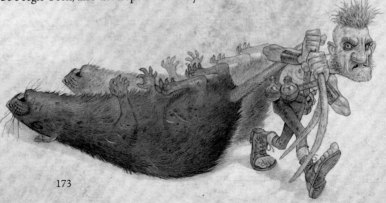

My dead rats have also developed over the 30 years I've found myself illustrating them – there really is nothing like practice!

173

"HOLLYWOOD COME IN ... YOUR TIME IS UP
TRAINSPOTTING IS HERE AND IT'S TOE-CURLINGLY GOOD"
★★★★★
EMPIRE

#1 BEGBIE #2 DIANE #3 SICK BOY #4 SPUD #5 RENTON

Trainspotting 18

From the makers of
Shallow Grave

CHANNEL FOUR FILMS PRESENT A FIGMENT FILM IN ASSOCIATION WITH THE NOEL GAY MOTION PICTURE COMPANY TRAINSPOTTING EWAN MCGREGOR EWEN BREMNER JONNY LEE MILLER KEVIN MCKIDD AND ROBERT CARLYLE AS BEGBIE INTRODUCING KELLY MACDONALD COSTUMES RACHAEL FLEMING PRODUCTION DESIGN KAVE QUINN EDITOR MASAHIRO HIRAKUBO DIRECTOR OF PHOTOGRAPHY BRIAN TUFANO B.S.C. BASED ON A NOVEL BY IRVINE WELSH SCREENPLAY JOHN HODGE PRODUCER ANDREW MACDONALD DIRECTOR DANNY BOYLE

SOUNDTRACK INCLUDES · DAMON ALBARN · BEDROCK FEATURING KYO · BLUR · ELASTICA · BRIAN ENO · LEFTFIELD · NEW ORDER · IGGY POP · PRIMAL SCREAM · PULP · LOU REED · SLEEPER · UNDERWORLD

If you would like to purchase this poster contact Carol Murray at Calton Athletic Recovery Group on 0141 5563449. All proceeds go to charity

anny Boyle's classic 1996 dark comedy *Trainspotting*, set in the underbelly of Edinburgh, had an iconic bold and graphic movie poster. The film is about a group of hardened Scottish friends battling adversity; in the poster they are presented without glamour or backdrop so their characteristics are first and foremost. I visualized the Nac Mac Feegles differently to those of Josh Kirby who drew them as muscle-bound Smurf types. I wanted to portray their tribal and gritty identity which was embodied in their tough and sinewy physicality. This is summed up by Ian Dury's remark when describing his own physical imitations, having suffered polio as a boy: 'It's not the size of the dog in the fight, it's the size of the

fight in the dog'. The Feegles are angry survivors despite being only six inches tall in a dangerous world, their fiery pictsie spirit has kept them alive. Somehow the parody struck me as apt not just in the perceived Scottish heritage of the Feegles, but because you wouldn't want to meet Rob Anybody down an alley after the pubs have closed any more than you'd want to meet Begbie.

Rob looked innocent, a sure sign of guilt.

WINTERSMITH

ROB ANYBODY

HAMISH

NOT–AS–BIG–AS–MEDIUM–SIZED–JOCK

FION

DAFT WULLIE

"FAIRYLAND COME IN . . . YOUR TIME IS UP

THE NAC MAC FEEGLES ARE HERE AND THEY'RE HEAD-BUTTINGLY GOOD"

★★★★★

Feeglespotting

From the makers of

Shallow Graves

CHAPTER EIGHT
GODS AND HEROES

COHEN
THE
BARBARIAN

I drew Cohen for the first time back in 1993, and that sketch was in the envelope I gave to Terry at the book signing. My starting point for the design was inspired by Leonardo da Vinci's anatomical study of an old man. It showed his sinuous muscular body, aged but still active. Cohen has decades' worth of battle experience and is loath to lay down his sword; it was that attitude I wanted to capture. The test was to illustrate a man in his eighties yet make him appear formidable. In a strange quirk of coincidence, I later met a fan who wanted to show me his Kidby Discworld tattoos. He stripped off to reveal a physique that was so like my drawing of Cohen it was remarkable; topped with his shaven head and white beard the resemblance was uncanny. He allowed me to photograph him for future reference (thanks Kev). When I next met him at a convention Kev had fully embraced his inner Cohen, complete with eyepatch and leather loincloth.

I always enjoy imagining how the characters would have looked when younger. Cohen in his prime has a thick muscular neck and a full head of hair. He is handsome, despite the eyepatch, and he was a definite hit with the ladies. I illustrated this at top speed for a wanted poster when we constructed Evil Harry Dread's Shed of Doom.

A further inspiration for the physical design of Cohen came unexpectedly one evening while watching *Gardeners' World* on the BBC. They interviewed an older gentleman who gardened with his top off. He was aged but muscular in a scrawny way. It just goes to show that you never know when inspiration will strike!

I have a very soft spot for Nijel the Destroyer (and Cohen's biggest fan) in his woollen vest. My own mum was a knitter so I feel his pain (and itching). I like his youthful optimism which overrides his lack of strength, charisma and skill. I gave him a classic barbarian necklace to accompany his oversized leather battle gear.

Cohen had heard of fighting fair, and had long ago decided he wanted no part of it.

THE LIGHT FANTASTIC

INNE JUSTE 7 DAYS I WILLE MAKE YOU A
BARBEARIAN HERO!

COHEN THE BARBAREAN

Nijel refers frequently to his barbarian instruction manual allegedly written by Ghenghiz Cohen and featuring the author with adoring women on the cover.

 based this painting on the 1982 iconic movie still of Arnold Schwarzenegger playing Conan the Barbarian. Whilst the film version shows Conan in the muscular prime of life, an all-powerful conqueror, my version shows the aged Cohen upon his throne at the start of *The Last Hero*. His battle-worn physique is scrawny and scarred and his posterior rests upon a cushion for his piles. He is bored after conquering the Agatean Empire and, despite encroaching old age, his attitude remains fearless and angry.

In my painting Cohen is primed ready for his last great adventure.

'How about you, Cohen?' said Evil Harry. 'I heard you were an Emperor.'

'Sounds good, doesn't it?' said Cohen mournfully. 'But you know what? It's dull. Everyone creepin' around bein' respectful, no one to fight, and those soft beds give you backache. All that money, and nothin' to spend it on 'cept toys. It sucks all the life right out of you, civilisation.'

THE LAST HERO

Boy Willie · Caleb · R. Saveloy · Cohen · Truckle · Old Vincent · Mad Hamish

My very first illustration of the Silver Horde in 'The Pratchett Portfolio'. It predates by five years 'The Last Hero' where I returned to these characters and developed them further. However, their basic characteristics remained the same, despite Terry remarking that there were too many wrinkly knees.

THE LAST HERO

In 1999 Terry and Gollancz commissioned me to illustrate a novella, *The Last Hero*. This was to be a Discworld fable with full-colour illustrations in a genre-blurring publication somewhere between graphic novel and illustrated book, a concept that was ahead of its time, as in those days adult illustrated books were not widely known as they are today.

It tied in with a house move and my first ever studio space. To mark the occasion and somewhat excited by the whole idea I embarked on a series of large-scale oil paintings, each measuring over four feet tall. In hindsight this was not good time management planning or the best way to navigate the huge expectations, workload and deadline.

During the two years of working on this project I also illustrated two Discworld Diaries, a calendar and *Nanny Ogg's Cookbook*. I was overstretched and pushed for time. *The Last Hero* was published in 2001, it became a bestseller and has been in print ever since. I still feel slightly sweaty when I look at it.

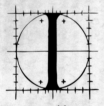

The omniscope is described as a type of magical magnifying glass that sees everywhere. I based my design on a scientific instrument in an old Christie's catalogue that I found on a stall amongst the chutney and knitted toys at Mells Daffodil Festival.

Kring the sword is in the Minstrel's scabbard singing the harmony.

The Minstrel's Lament was painted in acrylic towards the end of my illustrating marathon. That same year I was listening to Joe Strummer sing 'The Minstrel Boy', an Irish song written by poet Thomas Moore (1779–1852). The lyrics resonated with me and seemed to fit with Terry's description of the young minstrel who experiences a transformative journey to become a warrior bard by the end of The Last Hero.

The Minstrel-Boy to the war is gone,
In the ranks of death you'll find him;
His father's sword he has girded on,
And his wild harp slung behind him.

I think of it as my best work in the book. Sometimes, very rarely, it just happens:

When you're in the studio painting, there are a lot of people in there with you – your teachers, friends, painters from history, critics . . . and one by one if you're really painting, they walk out. And if you're really painting YOU walk out. – Philip Guston

I love painting mountains, and hope one day to do it en plein air. A wish I once shared with Terry and he assured me it would happen. One day I'll find the time . . .

raughtsman and designer of the
Renaissance, Michelangelo was born in Italy
in 1475 and early became known as an artist
whose painting and sculptures surpassed
those of antiquity. The commission to paint
The Creation of Adam, on the ceiling of the Sistine Chapel, took
him only four years despite the fact that the fresco covers 5,700
square feet. He completed all the work himself, only allowing
his assistants to conduct the menial tasks. He must have
suffered with terrible shoulder ache as he painted standing on
scaffolding with his brush held above his head.

My parody is a tongue-in-cheek tribute to this masterpiece. It
is one of the most replicated religious paintings of all time, so I
thought I would add one more version. Mine features the gods
with Blind Io stretching out his right hand to Cohen the elderly
barbarian, who, feeling perturbed by his mortality and angry at
the immortality of the residents of Dunmanifestin, offers the
finger as an act of octogenarian barbarian defiance. I felt this
painting summed up the whole theme of *The Last Hero*.

HIC TRAHVNT NAVES AD MARE

he original Bayeux tapestry is one of the most famous pieces of medieval art. It was embroidered in the eleventh century, around 1076. The cloth is 224 feet long and depicts seventy scenes of the events leading up to the Norman Conquest, culminating in the Battle of Hastings. Details include Halley's Comet and King Harold being struck in the eye with an arrow. The pictorial style of the original tapestry reminds me of a comic strip – one of my favoured methods of storytelling as a child, so naturally I was always inspired by it.

My version is a prelude to *The Last Hero*. It shows Cohen looking bored on the throne of the Empire he has conquered. It then depicts the Silver Horde setting off on their quest to return fire to the gods. Along the way there are depictions of kidnapping the Minstrel and Boy Willie losing his fight with a Walrus.

I drew more of the tapestry at the end of the story which shows Cohen and the Silver Horde stealing the Valkyries' horses and setting off to conquer new worlds.

THE GODS

T he gods of Discworld are wildly varied, ranging from Testudinidae to the cat-headed.

As Chief of the Gods, Blind Io bears a literary resemblance to Odin, Zeus and hammer-wielding Thor. I therefore illustrate him as a powerful deity with a strong physique in a classic Greek-inspired toga-wearing style. I looked at the work of two of my art-heroes, Frederic Leighton and Lawrence Alma-Tadema, who both had a penchant for painting togas (and other things). I also gave him a belt buckle and gold arm cuffs with a lightning-bolt-and-eyeball motif.

The Ephebian philosopher Abraxas is a toga-wearing agnostic who has been struck by lightning fifteen times. I paint him looking resigned to multiple singeings but still unshakeable in his beliefs.

You know where you are with big-brained monsters, but gods are another matter.

THE DARK SIDE OF THE SUN

Offler, the six-armed crocodile-headed god of Klatch, can sometimes manifest with two arms, which is how I have illustrated him here (saves on paint). I have included an egret with him not only because it's an excuse to paint a bird, which we have already established is something I love to do, but also because bird and reptile have a symbiotic relationship in real life, where the bird provides a dental hygiene service by picking debris from the crocodile's teeth.

Nuggan is described as tetchy and an inflexible stickler for rules. His Book of Nuggan forbids many of life's pleasures (chocolate, cheese, shirts with six buttons etc.), which he denounces as abominations. My illustration shows him hiding a Blind Io disguise behind his back in order to win over his followers.

My main goal when illustrating the Great God Om was to capture an air of grumpiness. He is frankly rather fed up with his lack of believers. I had a comment from a reader that his shell was not battered enough when I first drew him, so in my later painting I made sure he looks suitably knocked-around.

'He says gods like to see an atheist around. Gives them something to aim at.'

SMALL GODS

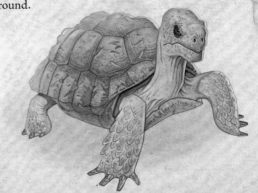

'I . . . think *my name is Bilious. I'm the . . . I'm the oh God of Hangovers.'*

'There's a God of Hangovers?'

'An oh god,' he corrected.

HOGFATHER

DISCWORLD PARODY: BACCHUS

he original opulent baroque masterpiece was painted in oils by the 24-year-old genius reprobate Caravaggio. It features a rosy-cheeked Italian libertine who languishes draped in a sheet on a couch whilst holding a crystal glass of wine. His head is wreathed in vine leaves and grapes and before him is a bowl of decadent fruits and a carafe of more red wine. The painting perhaps hints at the futility of decadent hedonism. Caravaggio himself was well versed in excesses. His drunken fiery temper often got him into fierce fights, on one occasion started by his artichokes being dressed in butter rather than olive oil. In 1606 he went beyond pub punch-ups and street brawling when he killed a man in a duel. He then had to become a fugitive for the remainder of his short life.

My version is a portrait of Bilious, the Oh God of Hangovers. It is based on the imagining of Caravaggio's youth a few hours after he enjoyed his wine . . . and the ensuing regrets. The name Oh God comes from the first thing that a person utters when waking up 'the morning after'. Nestled amongst the vine leaves around the sufferer's head is the merciless Headache Imp wielding a wooden mallet. The young man holds a glass containing, not wine this time, but a headache cure concocted by the wizards of Unseen University. Its ingredients include raw eggs, fresh orange juice, mustard and horseradish in cream with anchovies, yoghurt, willow bark, Englebert's Enhancer and Wow-Wow Sauce. In the illustration I have tried to capture a sense of nausea and regret in his expression and the trepidation about the effects of drinking the cure.

 his is my interpretation of one of the major works of Discworld art by 'a bloke with three i's in his name'. Anoia is described by Terry as a skinny, tired-looking woman draped in a sheet and smoking a sparking cigarette as a nod to her former career as the goddess of volcanoes. This brought to my mind Botticelli's *The Birth of Venus*, painted in 1484. The epic Renaissance painting features the goddess Venus standing upon a mythical scallop shell, which symbolizes fertility. In my version Anoia stands, in a nonchalant pose, in a rather more mundane cutlery drawer. In place of the roses, signifying love, that float in the air around Venus, are a plethora of kitchen implements including a ladle and a hand-whisk (notorious for getting jammed in drawers). I visited Botticelli's version in Florence years ago and got told off by a guard for getting too close.

Carefully placing cutlery by hand to work out the best placement is much easier than constantly re-drawing errant forks.

The desperate mad rattling and cries of 'How can it close on the damn thing but not open with it? Who bought this? Do we ever use it?' is as praise unto Anoia. She also eats corkscrews.

GOING POSTAL

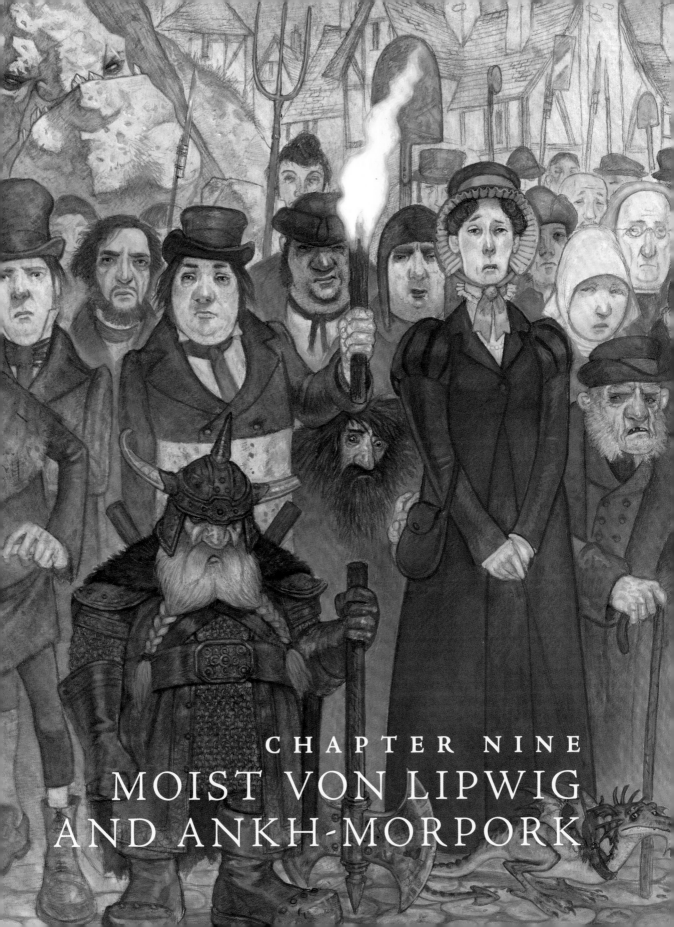

CHAPTER NINE
MOIST VON LIPWIG
AND ANKH-MORPORK

C.M.O.T. DIBBLER

I dress Dibbler in the type of garb one might find on the streets of Dickens's London. His clothes are ragged and mostly brown, even his shirt which started life as white. I took visual prompts for his look from the book *Gustave Doré's London* whose highly detailed engravings depicted people living in deprivation in Victorian times.

In my early drawings Dibbler's hat is felted wool in a medieval style; latterly I give him a nattier battered top hat which I think suits him. His scrappy neck scarf accentuates his scrawny neck.

C.M.O.T DIBBLER'S
PERSONAL GUARANTEE: IF YOU'RE INCINERATED
YOU GET YOUR MONEY BACK, NO QUIBBLE
ANTI-DRAGON CREAM

Don't forget to put the toilet seat down. (Consult 'The Truth' for eye-watering details.)

He has a hopeful, if shifty, smile as he desperately searches for the next retail opportunity. Terry describes him as having some rodent ancestry which I have taken into account by giving him small eyes, a long nose and small ratty ears.

Terry talks about different Dibblers appearing across the Disc, though Lobsang Dibbler (right) is only Dibbler himself in a disguise, hawking dubious remedies, allegedly from foreign lands. I'd like to draw the others some day.

196

He was extremely good at listening. He created a kind of mental suction. People told him things just to avoid the silence.

SOUL MUSIC

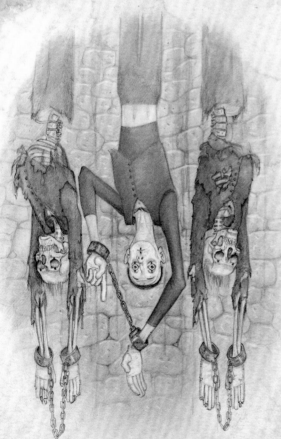

Vetinari has banned street theatre; my drawing imagines the consequences for those that flout the law. It appeals to my more macabre side.

LORD VETINARI

D escribed as a predatory black flamingo by Terry, I dress him in an austere Italian Renaissance outfit as a nod to Machiavelli. His neatly trimmed beard and tidy hair help to show a man with a liking for absolute order.

This artwork of Vetinari painted for *Guards! Guards!* places him inside his dungeons in the Patrician's Palace. Such austere surroundings actually suit him much better than the rest of the opulent building he usually inhabits. The ribbed vaulted ceiling is based on photographs I took one freezing January day at Netley Abbey, near Southampton.

MOIST VON LIPWIG

S ince he is described as a fraudster and habitual liar, I illustrate Moist with a likeable face, a necessity for a successful swindler. He has no particular outstanding features which enables him to easily adopt different disguises. Despite being good-looking, he is unmemorable. I designed a face with symmetrical proportions, known as golden ratio, which research has shown people have a preference for. As he does not have any strong facial features, he is actually quite challenging to draw in an engaging way.

POST OFFICE

My group portrait of the postal workers includes Miss Maccalariat, Senior Postman Aggy, Junior Postman Groat, Stanley, Mr Pony, Tiddles the cat and various Golems including Gladys and Mr Pump. They all stand behind a resplendent Moist wearing wingèd hat and boots.

I took my visual inspiration from a sepia photograph of mail carriers from the early 1900s.

NEITHER RAIN NOR SNOW NOR GLO M OF NI T CAN STAY THESE MES ENGERS ABO T THEIR DUTY

GOING POSTAL

ANKH-MORPORK POST OFFICE

A long time ago in a galaxy far, far away...

STAR WARS

TWENTIETH CENTURY-FOX Presents
A LUCASFILM LTD. PRODUCTION
STAR WARS
Starring MARK HAMILL · HARRISON FORD · CARRIE FISHER
PETER CUSHING
and
ALEC GUINNESS
Written and Directed by GEORGE LUCAS Produced by GARY KURTZ Music by JOHN WILLIAMS

[Miss Maccalariat's] hair was plaited an coiled up on either side of her head in those discs that bac home in Uberwal had been called 'snails' but in Ankh Morpork put peopl in mind of a woma with a curly iced bu clamped to each ear

GOING POSTAL

Miss Maccalariat has the sam
hairstyle as Princess Leia.
The similarities stop there

hen I designed the book jacket for *Going Postal*, Terry's 33rd Discworld novel, I loosely based it on the movie poster created in 1977 by Tom Jung for *Star Wars*, which itself owes a debt to classic Frank Frazetta designs.

Star Wars was for me, like many of my generation, an important part of my cultural DNA growing up. It was therefore a fitting opportunity to pay tribute. My version places Moist on a mountain of letters adopting the hero pose similar to Luke Skywalker. Where Luke holds his lightsaber aloft, Moist brandishes a letter. Also featured are Adora Belle Dearheart taking the position of Princess Leia, and, in plac of the droids R2-D2 and C3-PO, Tolliver Groa and Apprentice Postman Stanley. Behind them burn the clacks towers.

I created the soft blue glow around the moon adding colour pastel pencil to the painting.

ANATOMY OF A COVER

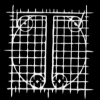

The cover for *Raising Steam* started as another complicated brief from Terry. Once again, just like *Snuff*, it initially included chickens. I drew an early version of a steam locomotive driven by Moist in a Victorian-style top hat. I kept the eyeline low to increase the drama.

Following feedback from Terry I changed the style of the engine to a more updated model. I also flipped the image horizontally from right to left and changed the eyeline to above rather than below because Terry requested that I show the train snaking off through a tree-lined rocky ravine with a troll on guard at the back.

He also asked that I add flying axes and a dwarf beside Moist.

On submission of my third rough, following more feedback from Terry, the dwarf had been swapped for a goblin and Moist now wore more practical train driver attire.

Once it had Terry's approval the next stage was to submit it to the publishers for the designers to position the lettering within the composition.

I then produced a small colour rough in watercolour to work out the palette. I chose complementary greens and oranges.

Having transposed my drawing onto illustration board I commenced painting, beginning with a detailed underpainting in raw umber acrylic.

Note the taped-on extra paper on the second version!

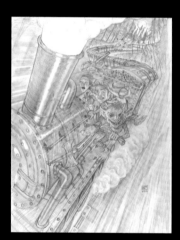

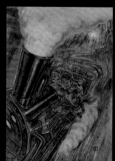

Goblin mechanics for the back cover, one of whom reminds me of a former colleague from my days working in the dental laboratory.

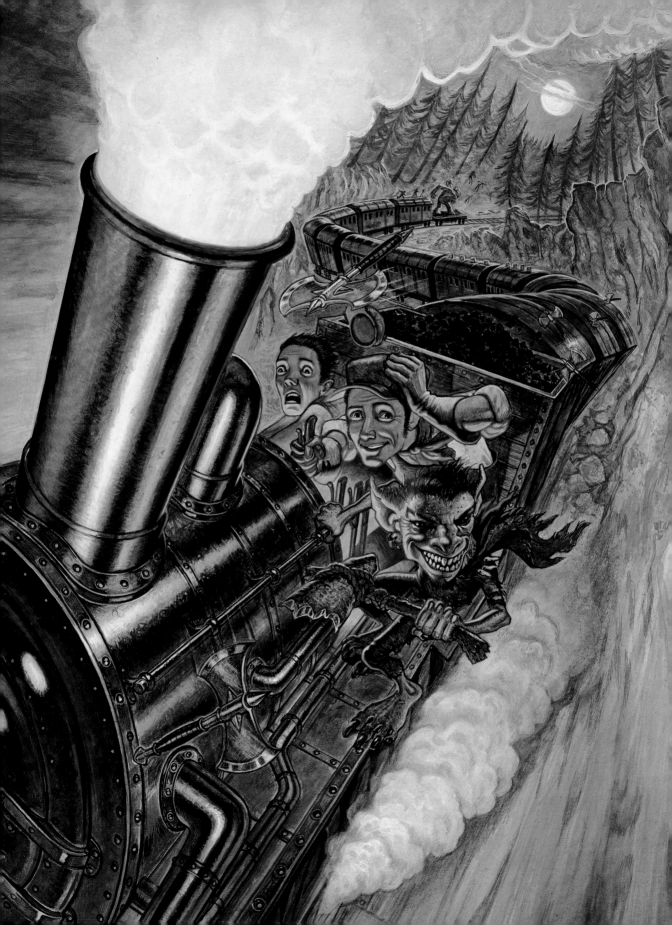

NON-HUMANS

I was talking to someone at a Discworld signing who worked in a mental health unit. He told me that they have the Fresh Start Club print on the wall of the clinic and that it made their patients smile. I like to hear stories of how my work can be meaningful to others, and bring humour to people who might be experiencing difficult times. The Fresh Start Club, like so many of us, are neurodiverse.

I paint Ludmilla and Mrs Cake wearing the sort of costume found in Jane Austen novels, as a werewolf in a poke bonnet is too good an opportunity to pass over.

'Brother Ixolite is probably the only banshee in the world with a speech impediment, so instead of sitting on roofs and screaming when people are about to die he just writes them a note and slips it under the door—'

REAPER MAN

Oooo Eeee Oooo Eeee Oooo EEEee

DOGS

I love dogs and opportunities to draw them.

Gaspode is the cleverest dog in Discworld, and he can talk. I draw him maintaining humanistic eye contact and with his mouth open as if to speak. I also try to portray the fact that he *'smells like a privy carpet'*.

We used to have a King Charles spaniel; by the time she came into my life she was food-focused and middle-aged. Her crowning glory was to be drawn for the *Discworld Post Office Diary* as one of the dogs with orange eyebrows.

Their names were Thunder and Lightning and they moved so fast, they set the air on fire and their coats outshone the sun . . .

A HAT FULL OF SKY

I illustrate Granny Aching's sheepdogs as intelligent Welsh sheepdogs with their focus on a distant flock.

eter Blake and his then wife Jann Haworth created the ground-breaking cover art for the Beatles' eighth studio album, *Sgt. Pepper's Lonely Hearts Club Band*, released in 1967. It has been much loved and parodied over the years. The original features a colourful collage of famous people from the worlds of fashion, film, art, literature and mysticism. Creating a denizens-of-Discworld rendition was too tempting a prospect and so I painted it for the 2012 calendar. Terry

This is also a story abo
sex and drugs and Mus
With Rocks In.

Well . . .

. . . one out of three
ain't bad.

SOUL MUSIC

THE GUILD OF
FOOLS

The Fools' Guild is one of the areas of Ankh-Morpork where Terry could immerse himself in history – which in this case is a perfect example of truth sometimes being stranger than fiction.

Doctor Whiteface was based by Terry on the Pierrot clown. Pierrot dates back to the seventeenth century, when he appeared in the Italian *commedia dell'arte*. Watteau was the first artist to paint him and he has reccured in artworks ever since. This is because he has become a symbol and alter ego for artists including Picasso, Seurat and David Bowie, who all related to his outsider persona.

My version is actually one of the scariest characters I have drawn to date. He has cold joyless eyes and a thin downturned mouth. His expression is in stark contrast to his Pierrot clown outfit which just accentuates his dark demeanour. I always feel sorry for his two pugs and so I draw them with worried expressions (which pugs do in fact have).

The coat of arms for the Fools' Guild contains a nod to music hall comedians of yesteryear ('dico dico dico' is dog Latin for 'I say, I say, I say'), and the painted eggs showing clown faces reference the Clown Egg Register – a real practice by which real-world clowns have their distinctive make-up recorded on eggs.

Every now and again I embark upon a group portrait with great enthusiasm. It takes me a few weeks of drawing by which time I vow never to do another – until the next time ...

In this illustration showing the heads of the Guild of Fools, I portrayed fifteen Fools' Guild officers in their various costumes. I take back what I said about Doctor Whiteface being the scariest of my creations when I look at Brother Bellwether (bottom row second from left), who is clearly the stuff of a fevered cheese dream.

No clowns were funny. That was the whole purpose of a clown. People laughed at clowns, but only out of nervousness. The point of clowns was that, after watching them, anything else that happened seemed enjoyable.

MEN AT ARMS

An invaluable component to a dangerous routine – invisible ferrets.

THE GUILD OF ASSASSINS

The Assassins' Guild badge. The alchemic symbols upon it are for poisons. The dog Latin motto translates as 'No killing without payment'.

only were his portraits an example of incredible draughtsmanship, they were also a valuable record of fashion.

I also admire the tenacity of Ingres, who during times of financial hardship would draw pencil portraits for 40 francs apiece, with his barber acting as agent. He did around 300 of these.

I designed Lord Downey with a long face and a friendly demeanour, which the unsuspecting would be inclined to trust and accept a humbug from. His clothing is respectable and smart with a high collar, cravat and a stovepipe hat in the fashion of an upright late Georgian gentleman – the type one might find in the pages of a Jane Austen novel.

> The members of the Guild of Assassins considered themselves cultured men who enjoyed good music and food and literature. And they knew the value of human life. To a penny, in many cases.
>
> HOGFATHER

All my depictions of the Assassins take inspiration from the pencil portraits by French artist Jean-Auguste-Dominique Ingres. He captured the likenesses of diplomats, composers and other gentlemen of merit, all dressed in fine French tailoring, at the turn of the 1800s. Not

A Sumtri Fire Newt, banned from the Assassins' Guild for obvious reasons. This one is eating a master, which is frowned upon (by other masters).

Another of my group portraits. On the far right is Alice Band. She began as a lesser character in a Discworld Diary and went on to become a lesser character in the novels. She bears a resemblance to Lara Croft in the writing, which is why I gave her little round glasses.

All assassins had a full-length mirror in their rooms, because it would be a terrible insult to anyone to kill them when you were badly dressed.

PYRAMIDS

The Wiggy Charlie weathervane graces the rooftop of the Assassins' Guild; in an example of life imitating art it also now graces the roof of The Chapel, Terry's former workplace and headquarters of the Pratchett Estate.

211

VAMPIRES

Count Bela
de Magpyr

Count de Magpyr

T he vampires of Discworld allow me to tap into my misspent youth watching Hammer Horror movies late at night and collecting the Comedy of Terrors: Hammer Horror Trading Cards. Every pack contained three cards, each with a truly awful joke, and one stick of chewing gum.

My association with vampires continued when I left school and worked in the dental laboratory making false teeth. And what young apprentice would be able to resist fashioning pairs of vampire fangs?

My designs for the Discworld vampires are always neatly groomed, self assured and rather suave.

Count de Magpyr, who has white streaks in his black hair as a visual reference to the magpie, and his uncle, Count Bela de Magpyr, wear evening dress ready for a night on the tiles . . .

Dragon King of Arms is described as having suspicious shoulders beneath his cloak that might possibly be folded wings.

Count Volosu
was famously
eaten by
Greebo.

Vampires have risen from the dead, the grave and the crypt, but have never managed it from the cat.

WITCHES ABROAD

212

REFORMED VAMPIRES

My illustrations of vampires that have taken the pledge and forsworn the dreadful consumption of human blood look somewhat fraught.

I have drawn John Not-A-Vampire-At-All Smith (left) with beads of sweat upon his brow, bloodshot eyes, ruffled hair and an expression of enforced jollity. The bite marks in his pipe, apple and teacup say it all.

The most well-known member of the League of Temperance is Otto Chriek. His name bears a similarity to the actor Max Schreck who starred in the silent German expressionist vampire film *Nosferatu: a Symphony of Horror* in 1922. The film was inspired by Bram Stoker's *Dracula* and had to be subsequently destroyed because the makers did not have copyright permission. Luckily a few copies remain and it is now regarded as a cult classic.

I enjoyed designing Otto's iconograph apparatus, with an imp, a jolly bat in place of a birdie and the salamander to provide the flash.

Bob is a member of the League but is actually not a vampire. They let him stay, feigning ignorance, because he's the only one who can tune the harmonium. Terry described him as looking like the Nosferatu Vampire.

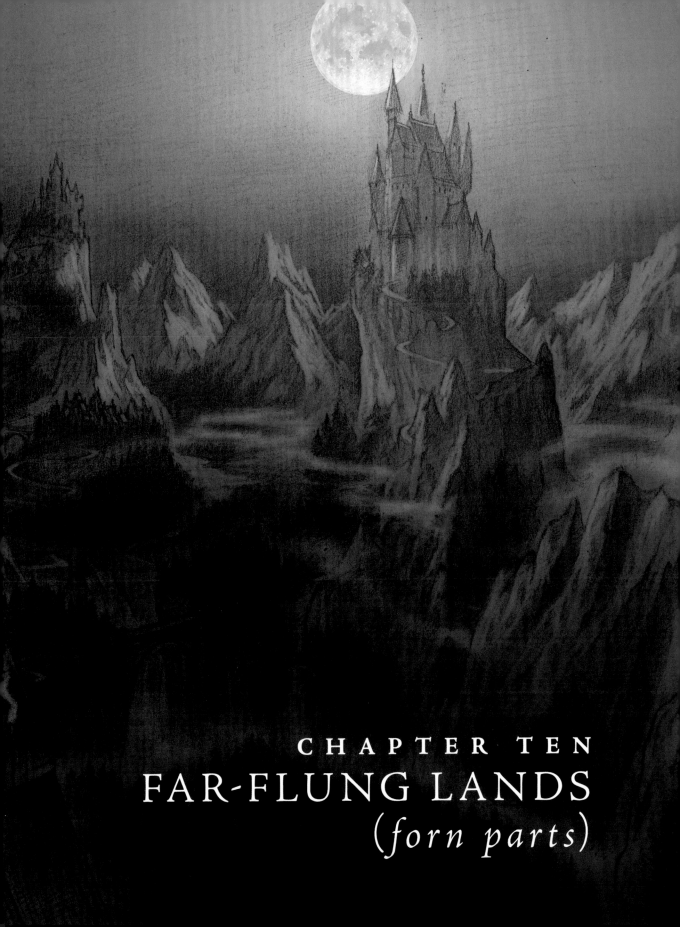

CHAPTER TEN
FAR-FLUNG LANDS
(forn parts)

THE AMAZING MAURICE

Sardines the dancing rat has a splendid set of false teeth (not his own). Once again my apprenticeship in the dental lab proved invaluable.

I particularly enjoyed designing the disgruntled Maurice. He is a very different cat to Greebo despite them both being streetwise felines with a back history of scrapping. Maurice is a chunky, stripy tabby with frayed ears that reflect his battles past. He has markings around his eyes that make him look like a bandit – or Zorro. I try to show through his expression that he has a Machiavellian intellectual capacity that is superior to Greebo, and other cats.

It was very unusual for Maurice to feel sympathetic to anyone who wasn't Maurice. In a cat, that is a major character flaw.

THE AMAZING MAURICE
AND HIS EDUCATED
RODENTS

When I showed this painting to Terry he requested that I make the cat's expression more grumpy. Which I did. Original version above.

The band of rats each have a unique persona which was fun to capture with my pencil. Peaches is soft and silky, Dark Tan is larger and more scarred with miniature tools and ropes, Dangerous Beans is albino and more anxious, and head rat is Hamnpork who is scabby and old. I gave him a thick scaly tail which emphasizes his age.

And that, really, was it. You didn't need many rats for a plague, not if they knew their business. One rat, popping up here and there, squeaking loudly, taking a bath in the fresh cream and widdling in the flour, could be a plague all by himself.

THE AMAZING MAURICE AND HIS EDUCATED RODENTS

 have long been an admirer of the work of American artist Maxfield Parrish and his treatment of glowing evening light. His *Pied Piper of Hamelin* was painted for the Palace Hotel in San Francisco in 1909 and still hangs there, above the bar, today. I felt that Terry's version of the Pied Piper legend presented the perfect occasion to pay tribute to Parrish's work. In the original version, the piper leads the children away from their home town. In mine, Amazing Maurice, the mastermind of the Pied Piper scam, leads his educated rodents and the 'stupid-looking kid', Keith, towards Bad Blintz. For good measure, I have also placed the Death of Rats and Quoth the Raven in the tree.

After a few days of this, it was amazing how glad people were to see the stupid-looking kid with his magical rat pipe. And they were amazed when rats poured out of every hole to follow him out of the town. They were so amazed that they didn't bother much about the fact that there were only a few hundred rats.

They'd have been really *amazed* if they'd ever found out that the rats and the piper met up with a cat somewhere in the bushes out of town, and solemnly counted out the money.

THE AMAZING MAURICE AND HIS EDUCATED RODENTS

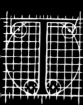his composition is based on Joe Rosenthal's photograph *Raising the Flag on Iwo Jima*. The title of Terry's novel takes its name from a sixteenth-century tract by John Knox opposing female rule, titled *The First Blast of the Trumpet Against the Monstrous Regiment of Women*, so it seemed apt for the cover artwork also to echo a past work. I have reversed the viewpoint so the group of female soldiers can be seen from the front.

Monstrous Regiment also sees the introduction of 'Fizz', the cartoonist for the *Ankh-Morpork Times*. Terry requested that I create a line drawing by him'. My cartoon is in the style of an etching by Hablot Knight Browne, whose pen name was Phiz. He is best known for creating illustrations for *Punch* and Charles Dickens, whose own

DJELIBEYBI

I have drawn Pteppic a few times over the years, but since my watching the *Mr Robot* series he took on an uncanny resemblance to Rami Malek. I give him a direct gaze and furrowed brow to portray his understanding of his predicament. Like all my Assassins he has high-end tailoring. He wears a silk hood and cravat and his cloak is fastened with a golden brooch featuring a scarab beetle holding the sun, which is a nod to his (unwanted) destiny.

Camels have a very democratic approach to the human race. They hate every member of it, without making any distinctions for rank or creed.

PYRAMIDS

'You Bastard' the camel. My challenge was to capture his sheer disdain.

Ptraci is described by Terry in *Pyramids* as having long dark hair. However, I have taken some artistic licence in my latest depiction of her and given her a Cleopatra hairstyle. She has the scarab beetle motif in her headband in reference to her regal lineage. Her expression is confident with a forthright look framed by classical Egyptian eyeliner. I enjoyed capturing a facial likeness between the (spoiler alert) siblings Pteppic and Ptraci.

OMNIA AND EPHEBE

Vorbis is a wholly unpleasant character, his physique exaggeratedly tall and thin. He is described as having skin stretched over bone, so I drew him with a pronounced domed head and sharp cheekbones to define his skull. His malevolent small, black eyes and long fingers add a sense of unworldly menace.

In contrast Brutha is not tall in stature and has a soft, rotund body and a gentle expression. Drawing him with big eyes helps to make him look more innocent.

> *'I used to think I was stupid, and then I met philosophers.'*
>
> SMALL GODS

Didactylos the philosopher is closely aligned with the Greek thinker Diogenes who, like his Discworld counterpart, lived in a barrel and carried a lamp in the daytime. I have drawn him with the scrawny body of someone more focused on thinking than eating. His wild beard and ragged robe emphasize his lack of focus on personal grooming.

> *Didactylos's thoughts chased after one another with a whooshing noise. No wonder he was bald. Hair would have burned off from the inside.*
>
> SMALL GODS

CHAPTER ELEVEN
OVER THE EDGE

CABBAGES AND KINGS

he artwork I get to create for Discworld is varied and sometimes delightfully esoteric. I've sketched, painted and sculpted creations both strange and sublime. Sometimes as little as a single line in Terry's writing will take me off on a potentially hilarious tangent. Other times, Terry himself will clearly be tickled by an idea and keep revisiting it across multiple books. Cabbages are one such peccadillo. The various members of the Brassica family evidently struck a chord with Terry, so the land surrounding Ankh-Morpork is fecund with cabbages (and the associated smell). Cabbages continue to appear in unlikely places and Terry even goes as far as describing the village of Big Cabbage, replete with a cabbage land theme park, a cabbage poet, cabbage beer . . . the mind boggles.

King Ludwig's four-year reign was one of the happiest of the entire monarchical period, and people looked forward to his proclamations on subjects such as the need to develop a new kind of frog and the way invisible creatures spied on him when he went to the lavatory.

THE ULTIMATE
DISCWORLD COMPANION

King Ludwig the Tree wears a ludicrous bejewelled crown and Georgian attire similar to monarchs past. I portrayed him with eyes looking in different directions, which is one of the expressions of Homer Simpson that I feel aptly displays a person caught up in their own confused inner world.

Perhaps the most amusing note I've ever received from a publisher was about the 'pig trick' illustration I created for *Tiffany Aching's Guide to Being a Witch*. I had carefully rendered a sausage with pig's legs, ears and curly tail. The feedback was that the illustration was wonderful, but 'undeniably phallic'. They weren't wrong. His nose was duly shortened. The original, er, grown-up version, hangs 'proudly' on the wall of Terry's office.

One of my fondest memories of going off on a fun tangent was creating the supernatural snowman for the back of *Wintersmith*. Terry approved of my Vitruvian Snowman design so much that he left a message on my answerphone to tell me so. It was the evil glowing eyes that really appealed to him.

A favourite of Terry's was the Castleman Hotel on Cranborne Chase. It used to have a painting on the walls named *Dead Fowl*, which depicted a pitiful collection of game birds painted in the old Dutch master style. However, it was the background which intrigued Terry and he made a point of delightedly showing me what he thought looked like a well-dressed Georgian couple being menaced by a werewolf. When I was working on some drawings for *The Discworld Almanak* in 2004 Terry gave me the title of a 'work of art' by Josiah Remnant and told me he was imagining it based on the Castleman painting. I was delighted to create the parody and, as a long-time vegetarian, I was very relieved to replace the dead birds with a selection of brassicas.

When I returned to this illustration in 2022 to paint a colour version I contacted the Castleman Hotel. They told me the painting no longer hangs in the restaurant but they did pass my request on to the owner who kindly sent me a photograph. We did some further research which led us to its likely artist, the Flemish Pieter Casteels III (1684–1749), who was born in Antwerp and trained by his father. He is largely known for his flower, game and bird scenes (and his occasional penchant for werewolves). He spent a significant portion of his life in England as a still life painter; his work was often found in country houses of the time (the upper classes seemed to have a strange fancy for surrounding themselves with paintings of dead game whilst they ate).

The apparent werewolf is not the only remarkable thing about this painting; I am also

amazed by the incongruous size of the poor dead fowl that is hanging from the tree – either the tree is very small or the bird is around thirty feet high. (I also like to think it is a potato on the far right.)

In homage to the original I have painted an absurdly large cabbage, namely the Rumptious Javelin, of which I know Terry approved.

It is for certain that the cabbage, which occupies most of the picture, was the prize-winning 'Rumptious Javelin', which weighed 295lbs and made three barrels of coleslaw.

THE DISCWORLD ALMANAK

Pablo the monkey came from *The Thieves' Guild Diary*. Terry gave me latitude to create artwork around which he would then write. One such addition was the Dodgeresque monkey on the back cover who was later named Pablo, though he never found a starring role . . .

   More often than not, a brief aside from Terry is fuel enough for a full-blown exploration of some of the most delightfully bizarre areas of Discworld.

   Terry delighted in forays about preposterous inventions. We had discussed the idea for Alice Band's exploding bustle in some depth and pondered its logistics before I commenced my design. I drew a cagelike receptacle, draped in fabric, that rolls along on four small wheels with a pedal-operated release mechanism. Terry was thrilled with the end result.

   Black Aliss, infamous witch on Discworld, gave me leeway to go – quite literally – 'warts and all' in a design. So much so, that when I illustrated her for *Tiffany Aching's Guide to Being a Witch*, I couldn't resist drawing a number of different shots of her, showing her 'descent into cackling'.

The joy of Discworld is its sheer range of subject matter. I mean, where else does an illustrator get to draw a frozen man in orbit? I looked at *The Body of the Dead Christ in the Tomb* by Hans Holbein as my starting point to design Mr Williams. I dressed him in eighteenth-century sailor's clothes rather than the loincloth of the old master painting and his face is set in frozen rigor mortis. It may seem a bit macabre but it's all in a day's work in the studio.

SPECIAL DELIVERY

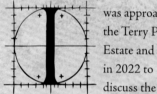

I was approached by the Terry Pratchett Estate and Royal Mail in 2022 to discuss the possibility of designing a set of special Discworld stamps to commemorate 40 years of Terry Pratchett's Discworld.

We drew up a longlist of favourite characters, and worked with Royal Mail to come up with our definitive eight. For some of the stamps, existing illustrations were the perfect fit, while artwork for Tiffany Aching, Death and Moist von Lipwig was specially commissioned.

The stamps had to work together as a cohesive set, with the characters being similar sizes and the layouts not too complicated – these are some of the smallest reproductions of my art ever made. Despite those constraints, it was still fun to include elements such as Rob Anybody on Tiffany's shoulder and the myriad details on the Moist stamp: the letter, featuring a Lord Vetinari stamp and addressed to 'My Brofer Jonn' (particularly fitting, as I have a brother called John), Worshipful Master Aggy's medal for facing aggressive dogs (15 bites and counting), and Junior Postman Tolliver Groat's doctor-repelling dead mole – the first such deceased talpid to ever feature on a stamp.

I pushed myself to finish the designs to the highest quality possible. The most difficult part of the process, however, was keeping the news to myself.

CHAPTER TWELVE

THE STUDIO
ENVIRONMENT

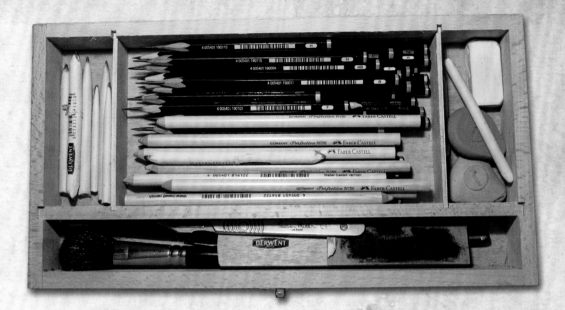

IN THE STUDIO

**P**eople are often surprised and perhaps a little disappointed when visiting my studio. It is not a jackdaw's nest of stuff, it is not paint-splattered or festooned with skeletons and it does not even have my art hanging on the walls. I did once have a painting framed and hung it over my workstation where it spent the morning, but by lunchtime I'd taken it down.

I keep the space as orderly as I can as it is not a large studio; it was originally a single garage which we converted just before the first Covid lockdown. It is painted white and is the lightest, brightest and most private space I have ever worked in. I keep my tabletop clean and free of paint, graphite dust, pencil shavings and eraser bits. I wipe it down every morning before I begin so my working surface stays clean. In many ways, with its empty walls and precision instruments, my studio is more akin to a laboratory – it is the other end of the scale to the working space of many artists, especially Francis Bacon.

Prior to working in this space, I spent many years without a studio at all. My illustrations were created at the dining table, with family life going on around me. I have been asked over the years why I don't have a separate building at the bottom of the garden, but my work is solitary enough without needing to physically remove myself from all human contact.

A valued companion and member of the studio team (alongside my wife) is our whippet. She either sleeps in a state of luxury under my table or alternatively chooses her fluffy donut bed for snoozing. She reminds me when it is time to stop and take a walk outside and when it is her supper time. In this space we also pack

My reference skeleton isn't real, but still lends the studio a certain macabre ambience . . .

and ship our website orders, do scanning and digital work and have our meetings. For a small studio it works very hard.

These days I generally stand to work at my height-adjustable desk unless I'm working on a large piece. Sitting for long hours gave me back problems and so for the last ten years I have done regular Pilates. For a few months I trialled sitting on a large yoga ball, but it was just too bouncy for fine detail work! There is also an armchair in the studio known jokingly as the therapy chair, as whoever sits in it seems to have an urge to unburden themselves. This is not to be encouraged …

I don't keep our large collection of art and reference books in the studio as there is not enough space, so these live in the smallest bedroom upstairs, rather grandly known as The Book Room. In the early days of my career there was no internet or digital photography and so I relied heavily on printed matter for reference resourcing. I would visit the library, photocopy pages, and gather imagery from magazines.

As previously mentioned, I am keen on geology. When I am out walking I have a tendency to scan the ground looking for interesting flints and fossils. I often bring examples home and my garden is full of them. This jar in the studio contains some of my favourites.

I collected the Dorling Kindersley Eyewitness Guides and books on all manner of topics from extraordinary chickens to Victorian country houses. Google images and my camera phone changed how I research for my illustrations, but I still like to refer to my book collection, particularly my art books for inspiration and to learn from the masters of art history.

Back in the days when my whippet studio assistant was a pup in training and I worked at the dining table and had to be careful of the carpet because the house was rented (flashbacks to my mum telling me off about plasticine in the carpet).

WORKING PROCESS

y method of creating artwork usually starts with ideas going into my notebook – often lists and written notes accompany the very rough and loose sketches. I never usually share these as they are just an extension of my personal inner processing. However, for the purposes of this book, I am showing some of the pages from my Moleskin collection.

Following the rough planning stage, I am then prepared to embark on a new illustration. As I have the concept planned in my head the pencil stage becomes a finished drawing without further sketches or working drafts. I start loosely and gradually refine and amend, taking lines out and putting them back in; my rough shading progressively becomes finer and the subjects gradually take form. I use my eraser as much as my pencil: the process is all about getting it wrong until I get it right.

In the old days I would then work in paint directly over my pencil drawing to create a sepia underpainting. Now I can scan the drawing and paint over a printout on board. This means the pencil drawing is no longer lost and I can refer to it as I paint.

I most often work happily in silence, but a Bluetooth speaker occasionally adds some relaxing ambience.

My tablet for easy access to my reference photos

Very sharp graphite pencils - I even use these on top of colour, for subtle shading.

The final stages of illustrating my Royal Mail special stamp design

MATERIALS

 ver the years I have experimented with all manner of mediums and equipment and enjoy exploring the new developments in media. Like all artists I love visiting the art shop and selecting new paints, papers and colour pencils and I don't skimp on these. In other areas my studio is not elaborate. I have a simple Ikea table and my chosen mixing palette is still an offcut of Formica that I salvaged from my dad's shed over thirty-five years ago. In short, if you have good quality materials such as quality brushes that will not shed hair on the work, pigment-rich paint and pencils and thick paper that will not cause frustration by buckling, then the other studio trappings are not really important.

PAINT

Whilst I love the rich vibrant luminosity of oil paint, for practical reasons (namely the drying time) the bulk of my work is painted in acrylics. I use the Winsor & Newton Professional range which does not colour shift from wet to dry and has a good working time in the palette.

More recently I have been combining my mediums to include Liquitex Acrylic Gouache paints. These have more opacity than acrylics and are good for blocking in dense areas of colour.

I have also recently added to my paint collection with watercolours. Sennelier and Daniel Smith both make high-pigment paint that produces vibrant colours. I like to create wash backgrounds allowing the hues to run into each other in an organic fashion. Some of the paints, such as DS Shadow Violet, produce secondary breakout tones. Allowing the paint to run freely on wet paper and create serendipitous effects is experimental, fun and a great antidote to my fine detail work.

When a painting is nearing completion, I sometimes use Caran d'Ache Luminance colour pencils for finishing touches, highlights and details.

I generally use Winsor & Newton Cotman brushes series 111 round which are good for fine detail, lines and washes, and their synthetic fibres maintain a good point. They are actually designed to be used for watercolours but as I use my acrylics very thinly, building up tones and colours in washes, they suit me well. However, I do go through them pretty fast. The smallest brush size is 0000, which I occasionally use for extra detailed details!

It's always helpful to have assistance organizing your materials!

Any day buying art supplies is a good day.

SURFACES

Back in the old days my drawing and painting surface of choice was always CS10 board. However, this went out of production years ago so I moved over to a similar option, Schoellershammer 4G Illustration Board (both were produced primarily for airbrushing). This, frustratingly, is also no longer produced and I scour the internet looking to buy old stock. I like it because it has a bright white smooth surface and allows precise pencil work with an easily erasable surface; it takes wet paint well and scratching back into the surface with a scalpel. It is ideal for drawing, watercolour-style acrylic, pen and ink.

I also use Breathing Color 300 gsm Pura Smooth from the US which is 100 per cent cotton archival fine art paper and comes on a roll so is ideal for large works such as *The Discworld Massive Massif*. This is dry-mounted with film onto mount board to provide a stable surface for painting on the easel. Thankfully this is still produced so sourcing is not an issue!

For smaller works on paper, I use Daler Rowney 250 gsm Graphic Series Bristol Board for drawing. This also has a bright white smooth surface with no texture.

Claybord is an American product which I discovered via the magic of Instagram. This is a museum quality panel that is very useful for black ink drawings. It is ultra-smooth and can take very fine lines and refinement with my scalpel. I produced all the chapter headings for the illustrated *Good Omens* on this surface.

A design on claybord, inspired by the etchings of Albrecht Dürer

PENCILS

My impressive pencil point has attracted attention in the past, so much so that I was once interviewed about it by a German doctor with a passion for stationery on his blog Bleistift.

When I draw, I use the Faber-Castell 9000 series in lead grades 3B, 2B, B, HB, F, H, 2H, 3H, 4H. My favourites are F and H. I don't use 3B, 2B or B very often because they can make my work go smudgy – so I save them for areas where it needs to be very dark. If I am shading, I work left to right on the page and protect the pencil drawing behind my hand with a clean sheet of paper to prevent smudging.

I use Derwent stumps for blending and Faber-Castell Perfection 7056 pencil erasers which I can sharpen to take out highlights in my drawing. More recently I have taken to using a battery-operated Eono refillable eraser which can produce very accurate highlights. I sharpen my pencils with a Swann-Morton DS2902 scalpel with 10A surgical blades, I then sand the pencil point using a Derwent sanding block. I sharpen to a long point because it gives me better control.

AIRBRUSH

Back in the old days of working for commercial studios my trusty airbrush saw a lot of action and my first flat (and its contents) had a fine coating of paint. After 35 years of service, I recently retired my old trusty rusty compressor and replaced it with a dinky Chinese IFOO. I now only airbrush occasionally; I bring it out when the weather is fine and use it in the garden where the chances of covering my studio (and my lungs) with a fine layer of paint are less. If am working with the toxic cadmium hues I wear a mask.

'Pomme the IV', a New Forest donkey

The fearsome Slasher, Steed of Terror, biter of fingers, and Evil Harry Dread's mount

INSPIRATION

When I am not actively in my studio working, I am still working! This is because my mind is constantly processing ideas and collecting visual inspiration. My iPhone is full of thousands of photos, mostly of the natural world around me and the animals I share my life with. My whippet and her lurcher predecessor can be found incarnated as dragons, likewise the ponies, donkeys and cattle of the New Forest. Animal facial expressions coupled with a tilt of the ears bring character and personality which translates easily from real life into the fantastical. I tend to collect wherever I go: digital photographs of clouds, seed pods and trees, and pocketfuls of flints, shells and twigs with lichen. Inspiration is everywhere if you remember to look!

I often find that the faces I know best creep into my work, therefore elements of my own features (drawn so often in the Miss Ockendon days), and those of my wife, tend to recur. All these factors are brought into the mix when I illustrate Discworld, but of course the greatest source of my inspiration is Terry's writing itself.

CHAPTER THIRTEEN
PERCHANCE TO DREAM...

THE ROAD NOT TAKEN

Collaborating over illustrations for his work, Terry was always generous about incorporating anything he considered a 'good idea'. He also didn't mind letting you know when you'd had a bad idea . . . but, of course, that was his right. Any artist will try to bring something of their own to a creative process, and I always relished the times when I could drop small thoughts and suggestions into pieces, and proud when Terry went with them.

Now that Terry is no longer with us, I try very hard to 'colour within the lines' and steer clear of approaches that I know would run counter to his sensibilities as I understood them. However, for this book, his estate suggested that it might be fun for me to take a first pass at designing some covers for the Discworld books that Terry never got around to writing, based on the ideas for stories that he had been talking about before time ran out on him.

It's a source of frustration and great sadness to all of us, of course, that we'll never get to hold and read these planned books. But we can at least – and I hope without presuming too much – imagine what they might have looked like had they made it into the world and onto our shelves.

THE BOY

A story in which an Ankh-Morpork urchin becomes archchancellor of Unseen University. Terry commissioned me to create this picture as a potential mood piece, which might eventually form a cover idea. Ultimately, the narrative tides took Terry elsewhere, but some passages of this unfinished book found their way into *Unseen Academicals*.

THE TURTLE STOPS

In this book, Great A'Tuin is dying. The wizards, having ascertained that the great star turtle is ailing by observing its motions from the very top of the Tower of Art (aided, we assume, by magical lensing at the edge of the Disc), decide to mount a rescue expedition into the creature's body, in an adventure reminiscent of *Fantastic Voyage*. As to crew: besides Ridcully and Ponder Stibbons, I felt an Igor would make a good vet, and Marchesa and the Krull Archastronomer would offer valuable Krullian insights into the whole chelonian mystery. Rincewind is there because this sort of thing always happens to him, and I included a moon dragon, because – and if you've been paying attention throughout this book, this won't surprise you – I really like dragons.

CLANG!

In *Night Watch*, the seminal Discworld novel about revolutions, Vimes notes that revolutions are so named because they come around again.

Terry loved folding obscure knowledge into his novels, and one strange corner of history he filed away for later use was campanology – the art of bellringing. Bells in medieval times would bring in workers from the fields – the perfect cover for sending covert but audible messages. There was practically nothing else to go on for this novel, but the concept conjures up images of classic French tales, and it's a small (silent) leap to get to mimes, the White Hand Gang, and other subversive elements present in Ankh-Morpork. Within the scene I got to include some of my favourite parts of this under-examined corner of Discworld, particular to the fools – balloon animals, boxes of invisible ferrets and sloshi warriors.

TWILIGHT CANYONS

In which the elderly patients in a home for the bewildered solve the mystery of the missing treasure and defeat the rise of the Dark Lord despite the fact that many of them don't entirely know whether it's Tuesday or a lemon.

This piece parodies *Napoleon Crossing the Alps* by Jacques-Louis David. Evil Harry Dread, of *The Last Hero* fame, would have taken centre stage, and, I assume, so would his trusty mount, Slasher, the steed of terror. Donkeys are long-lived, so it seemed a pleasing detail that even in his dotage, Evil Harry still has his grizzled, finger-biting, asinine companion.

CAB'S WELL

The concept here, as Terry explained it to me, was 'some poor bloke down a wishing well whose job it is to make wishes come true.' Some of Terry's very best stories can be summed up just as simply, but, of course, they become far more complex in the telling, which is the beauty of it. Either way, I've added a black cat. I can't imagine Terry ever arguing against the inclusion of a cat.

SCOUTING FOR TROLLS

When Terry penned 'Minutes of the Meeting to Form the Proposed Ankh-Morpork Federation Of Scouts', it was what he called 'a squib', a short written sketch that might one day spawn a longer story. (You can read the whole piece in *A Blink of the Screen*.) That story would most likely have been *Scouting for Trolls*, in which young Ankh-Morpork delinquents would have had their energies directed towards more wholesome pursuits. The title says it all. I've rarely had less need of further briefing. I like to imagine some of the badges on display are for such notable achievements as 'knot tying', 'constructive violence' and 'helping old ladies across the road'.

THE REDOUBTABLE MAURICE

The Amazing Maurice finds himself as a ship's cat. Beyond this certainty, Terry didn't specify what else would befall Maurice, but cat plus water immediately suggests a certain reaction on Maurice's part. A few other, more oblique nods to German folklore are also included in the picture.

I don't know if Maurice's educated rodents would have joined him – Terry wasn't overly prone to sentiment, but who knows; I don't think even he knew where stories would take him . . .

RUNNING WATER

Moist von Lipwig is riding high – until he's sent to a new low. Or actually, a very old one. Terry knew that Moist would eventually delve into the deep, dark places under Ankh-Morpork, where an older Ankh-Morpork lies forgotten, and another one under that. And those Ankh-Morporks would turn out not to be so dead after all . . .

Starting with the usual municipal focus, this time water, with a moustachioed* Moist cast as the Disc's Joseph Bazalgette, the novel would have involved Lord Vetinari's 'undertaking', with the underground expansion of the city as it hurtles into the future.

I decided that goblins would probably feature – not such a big stretch, given the cast of Terry's more recent Moist and City Watch books. I also included a gnoll, cast in a Father-Thames role here, a natural fit for the ever-more Dickensian underbelly of Discworld.

* A fake moustache, I'd warrant

THE FEENEY

A book following the adventures of Constable Feeney, first introduced in *Snuff*. It was suggested to me that this countryside tale might have ended up containing more violence than one suspected, hence the beartraps. The title is a nod to the 1970s John Thaw and Dennis Waterman police drama *The Sweeney*, while the composition is a homage to the poster for the 2013 Scottish crime comedy *Filth*, which also features its protagonist astride a pig. Why not?

UP SCHOOL!

'Susan becomes the headmistress of the Quirm College for Young Ladies'. Another simple one-line pitch that seems to suggest so much more when you have a longer think about it. Much of Susan's life is defined by the (often unwelcome) intervention of her grandfather and his associates. I took a few days contemplating how this one might have looked, but once you get to Death wearing a mortarboard cap, you pretty much have it.

AFTERWORD

AND THE PATH AHEAD . . .

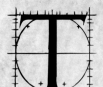erry's boundless imagination was constantly leaping ahead of him and he had multiple books on the go at any time. As his latest novel was being toured, he would be quietly working on the next passion project. And also on the one after that. And sometimes on the one after that, too.

Terry's plans for where Discworld would go next were always delicious to anticipate but impossible to predict. When he died, many of his collaborators were left holding small pieces of the roadmap. But what Terry hoped would unfold according to his plan, and what should be left untouched and sacrosanct, has always been crystal clear to his family and to us guardians of his literary estate. Terry certainly didn't want any new Discworld novels written after his death.

However, he had always eagerly anticipated a definitive guide to Discworld, something that, logically, would only be possible once he'd stopped writing the books. I guess you could think of it as a retirement project – except that Terry didn't do retirement, not even in the face of a debilitating illness. Given his drive and the dedication to the cause which kept him writing until it was impossible to write any more, that definitive guide could only possibly be assembled after his death. Terry always envisioned it taking a multi-volume form – a Discworld encyclopaedia, the kind of reference work that fascinated and inspired Terry in his childhood and throughout his life, taking the reader on a self-propelled browser's journey deeper and deeper into Discworld.

This book is the first move in that direction. It's my fervent hope that those encyclopaedia volumes will emerge in the years to come, giving Terry's artist of choice the continuing opportunity to illuminate every corner of Discworld while we carefully follow the course that Terry charted for us.

Rob Wilkins
The Chalke Valley
May 2024

PICTURE CREDITS

'a good honest potato'

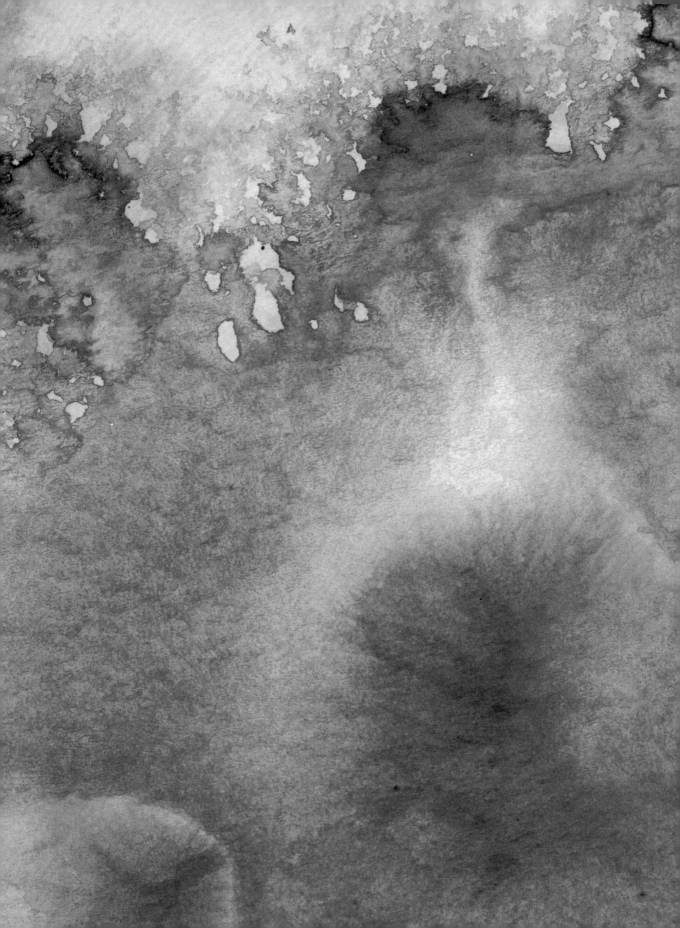